FOOTBALL
FOR
PLAYER AND
SPECTATOR

by
Fielding H. Yost

PREFACE

Between the covers of "Football for Player and Spectator" the author has endeavored to gather from his experience as a player and a coach the advice which is best suited to the needs of the young men in high schools, preparatory schools and colleges who desire to participate in the greatest of all the competitive athletic sports.

Acting on the principle that example is, after all, the very best teacher, an endeavor has been made to thoroughly illustrate the various positions, plays and formations, the photographs from which the reproductions have been taken being posed with this especial end in view.

As the title of the work implies, the book aims also to make the game plain to the spectator who may not have enjoyed the advantage of close acquaintance afforded the man who has taken an active part in the play on the field.

Above all, however, should a perusal of the work give the reader, be he player or spectator, an adequate idea of the spirit in which the game is both played and viewed in its best form, the author will feel adequately rewarded for his labor:

F. H. Yost.

ANN ARBOR,
SEPTEMBER, 1905.

CONTENTS

FOOTBALL

ITS ORIGIN AND DEVELOPMENT

Football, although indefinitely known as a sport to Greek and Roman antiquity, did not come into existence as a school or college game until the eighteenth century. During the three or four centuries prior to this time football, in a vague way, figured in English inter-town and county contests. It first appeared as a distinct school game in the early part of the eighteenth century, but at this time was in more or less disfavor on account of the strict Puritanism of the period.

It is to the English schoolboy that the game of football really owes its origin. During the middle of the nineteenth century there was an athletic revival throughout England and football became the favorite pastime of the winter months in such schools as Rugby, Eton, Harrow, Charterhouse and others. The game came to its present important position through a gradual evolutionary process in which both a standard of play and of rule were developed together. In the growth of the two principal forms of modern play, "Association" and "Rugby," the size of the particular school ground was the determining factor. In 1850 the only school playground in England large enough to permit the running and tackling game was connected with Rugby. At Harrow, kicking and fair catching were allowed. A game was developed at Eton peculiar to this school and called the "wall game," while at other schools the play consisted almost entirely of so called "dribbling," in which carrying the ball and tackling were unknown.

The two systems of play, outgrowths of environment,

have ever since retained their individuality, constantly increasing along well defined lines to the present day.

Originally each school was bound only by self-made rules. Not until 1863 was there any attempt at codification. At that time a number of Rugby clubs in London met and attempted the adoption of laws governing their play. During the next ten years several attempts were made by the exponents of the two forms of football to formulate a code which would unify the two systems. At this time the followers of the dribbling game greatly outnumbered their rivals, but, notwithstanding this fact, Rugby retained its individuality and the numerous attempts at consolidation were without success.

In 1871 the clubs of London met and agreed upon a code out of which the present Rugby game of England and the intercollegiate game of America developed.

Prior to this time, however, a crude sort of football was being played on this side of the ocean. As early as 1840 at Yale, contests resembling to a certain extent the early game at Rugby were in vogue between the freshman and sophomore classes. In reality this series of games was, however, little but the prototype of the modern class rushes which are prevalent in most colleges at the present time. The so-called football soon assumed so strenuous a form that the faculty at Yale was obliged to abolish the custom, and the game was not revived at this institution until the early seventies.

Through the influence of a Yale undergraduate who had previously attended Rugby, inter-class football games were inaugurated in 1873, under a modified system of Rugby Union rules. In the meantime the game was also being developed at other seaboard colleges in America. Harvard, Rutgers, Princeton, Columbia and others were doing their share toward its development. At first the contests were of an inter-class or inter-hall variety. In the progress of the play, however, the desire for intercollegiate competition grew, and in October, 1872, representatives of Yale, Rutgers, Princeton and Columbia met in New York and adopted a set of rules which formed the first intercollegiate football association in America.

While throughout the New England towns and villages at this period a "dribbling" game was being played, the American colleges naturally adopted a form of play resembling that in progress under the English Rugby rules. Running with the ball and tackling, in fact every feature which tends to make the game a vigorous one, have subconsciously moulded the game in America. College football in the United States now stands as an exemplification of the athletic instincts of its younger generation.

The assimilation of the Rugby game and its evolution into the form in which football is now played in the United States were matters of considerable time and no small amount of deliberation. The English rules were found to be ambiguous in some cases, and difficult of comprehension in others. The novelty of the game, also, was productive of many suggested alterations and it was one of these which is really accountable for the wide difference which now exists between Rugby and American football. This was the adoption of a clause which permitted the forwards to heel or pass the ball out from the scrimmage where it could be grasped by one of the backs, who could then advance it. This was a procedure not tolerated in the original form of the game, but the additional interest which it imparted was immediately seen and the superiority of this plan for putting the ball into play, over the English method of kicking it about in scrimmage, was so apparent that it was eagerly embraced.

Yale Field—Yale vs. Princeton.

In logical order then followed the selection of one man to do the passing, through the greater accuracy which was thus secured, and the alignment of the men in the forward positions, instead of the old form of helter-skelter. Naturally, the heavy men were grouped about the center to protect him and the man immediately behind who was to receive the pass, while the lighter and faster men were assigned to duty on the ends.

Other provisions of the English game were altered to suit the new conditions and a rules committee, composed of prominent sportsmen of the leading institutions where the game was played, made numerous other changes in finally placing the game on a uniform basis. But one kind of intercollegiate football is now played the whole country over, and of recent years the changes in the rules have been comparatively slight and unimportant. The desire of the men who have from time to time served on the committee has been to develop a game which is clean and manly, and only a reference to the present code of rules is needed to demonstrate the stringent penalties placed upon any tactics even bordering on the unfair. The safety of the individual players has always been carefully looked after by the committee and the most important change made in the rules in recent years was the abolition of the flying wedge and its variations of mass play, an action taken in 1894.

In recent years as well, the rule makers have been endeavoring with continued success to cultivate the attractive features of the game by bringing kicking and open field running into greater prominence, a purpose which is being steadily accomplished without the sacrifice of any of the former attractions which the game has always possessed for both player and spectator.

To a great extent the rapid progress of the game has

been due to the natural rivalry manifested between the
elevens in the various institutions which took up the game
at about the same time.   Since the very earliest days of
the game the contests between Yale and Princeton have
roused the interest, not only of the students and alumni, but
of a constantly increasing proportion of the sports-loving
public.   Yale and Harvard have maintained their annual
competition almost every year.   Pennsylvania has long been
one of the best known homes of the game.   West Point
and Annapolis, the national schools for army and navy
officers, have always been supporters of rival football teams.
Numerous other institutions, natural rivals, have assisted
in the development of the game, urged to increasing efficiency by the progress of the competitor, and the west has in
more recent years taken a position of enthusiastic support
until now the game is practically general in all parts of the
United States, not only in the colleges, but in preparatory
schools as well.

FOOTBALL

ITS PRESTIGE AND POPULARITY IN AMERICAN COLLEGES AND HIGH SCHOOL LIFE

The necessity which impelled the English schoolboy at Rugby a century ago to inaugurate some healthful, clean and interesting outdoor sport and the felicitous choice of this form of recreation are the factors which have caused the growth of football until now it is the leading college game of America. It originated in a simple, Anglo-Saxon desire for clean, energetic sport and the participants in the game were the only spectators. It lives now through the same desire, but the interest in the game has so developed that hundreds of thousands throughout the country annually witness its play, not as mere spectators but as ardent votaries. From Maine to California, from Minnesota to Texas, wherever there are schools or colleges, football, during the crisp, autumn days, is the magnet which draws people from every walk of life from offices and shops for a few hours in the open air.

History shows us that college life, before athletics had been so universally adopted, was very often a detriment to the physical development of the student. Formerly two ideals, diametrically opposed, met the student at his advent. There was the bookworm, with his high forehead and stooping shoulders on the one hand, and the gilded youth who sought and enjoyed the reputation of being the best billiard and card player in the institution, on the other. There was no middle course open to him if he aspired to distinction as a popular idol among the underclassmen. The billiard hall, with its poor light and poorer ventilation, or the stuffy card

Ferry Field, Michigan.—Chicago vs. Michigan.

room, where its peculiar accomplishments were taught, offered the gravest menace to the physical well being of the student at this most critical period of his existence. Nor was the life of the bookworm better in this particular.

This condition does not exist at the present time. Before the prospective college man has finished his preparatory course necessary to an entrance into the higher scholastic field, the college athlete, the football player, the nearest approach to the all-round man, is the central figure in his ambitious dreams. Into his visions of physical supremacy there has been dexterously inserted by his older brother, his father and his different school teachers the absolute necessity for study. He realizes and regards it more seriously than did his active, young prototype thirty years ago. He is imbued with the definite ambition and knows that, before its accomplishment can possibly be attained, he must, first of all, be the student.

During that period of life ordinarily spent in college, energy and vitality are generated so abundantly that some legitimate physical exercise of a strenuous nature must be invented as a safety valve. Improperly directed or neglected, this surplus of vitality works an irremediable damage to the after life of its possessor. It is a matter of speculation, of course, but is, at the same time, warranted by our knowledge of what athletics are doing at the present time, that many men of brilliant promise in their early college life of a century ago would have been prominent in football had they lived at the present time, and would have thus avoided many influences which, in some cases, undoubtedly ruined their careers of service to the world.

Objections to football have been heard in certain quarters on account of its alleged brutality and the violence of the exercise demanded in its play. It is certainly not a game for weaklings or improperly trained boys, but statistics show that accidents of a serious nature are no more frequent in football than in horseback riding, hunting, yachting and many other kindred sports, which do not meet with disapproval on this ground. The game is no more violent than is required by the physical demands of the men who play it.

There are no memories which cling so persistently to the mind of the alumnus, always capable of awakening a glow of enthusiasm and always recalled with pleasure, as those interwoven in the football games of his undergraduate days. There are no ties so potent to bind him to the college through the business of after years. The conversations at class reunions invariably drift to football in general and certain games in particular. A comparison of the present with the past, which makes the undergraduate and the alumnus one in spirit, is of necessity drawn in this way. It is loyalty to college—college spirit—which makes the college man a valuable addition to the institution he adopts. It is the self-same spirit or a sentiment that stands for the best in college life and is an absolute essential to its success in its highest meaning, and it is college athletics, of which football is the highest exemplification, which make this spirit possible.

Without athletics the college life is dull and listless and a man leaves the halls of his alma mater, an alumnus, with the relief attending an accomplished task.

But, at the same time, while sentiment and spirit are essentials to success in the life of every man, they cannot lie dormant and accomplish the desired results by their mere existence. In conjunction with them must go other just as valuable attributes and these attributes are fostered and developed in football as in no other known game. Self-reliance, moral courage, "sand," determination, energy, discipline, judgment, self-restraint and enthusiastic interest are all found in the successful football player.

The training the football candidate necessarily undergoes is never wholly forgotten and, in after years, when he has left college and is grappling with the problems of life, it is an inestimable advantage. The player must learn to act for himself and quickly. In the stress of the game he must draw from his own resources in all emergencies. An inclination to falter through timidity or fear of the consequences is a complete disability. He must have a definite object in view in every play and must carry it through with bull-dog tenacity. His own interests must be subservient to the interests of the team. He must carry his whole heart into every play of the game and must never lose his temper. These same rules, properly carried out, bring success in after life.

The same vital points, continually drummed into a player in his training, are sure to influence the spectators who daily gather on the field to witness the practice. These attributes, personified in the ideal football player, dominate the entire student body and create a spirit which reaches out from the athletic field through the campus and into the very recitation room. The influence for good exerted in this way is incalculable.

In many cases students who would otherwise have been failures from the standpoint of physical development have been fired by the example of the football player and have developed ability which has been used for the glory of the college and the physical welfare of the owner in after life. The example of self-sacrifice engendered on the football field often extends in most surprising ways to the entire student body, and even those not participating in the active

THE STADIUM—HARVARD vs. YALE.

Photo by Burr McIntosh.

athletics are moved to habits of temperance and regularity. The perseverance which eventually brings success on the football field is an open book to every member of the undergraduate body and points the way to both athlete and student, not only during the college days but later in life as well. Independence of action and quickness of thought are sharpened by active participation in the game. Almost every college man is a conscientious and studious follower of the game. In no way is the utter futility of incompetence better illustrated than on the football field.

Aside from the better physical health resulting from a few hours spent on the field as spectators of the daily practice or the regular contests, the students return to their books or recitations with a mental exhilaration which is of great assistance.

From the opening of college in September, in all sections of the country, to its close in June, football is the most potent factor in the moulding of spirit, in the making of men, and in the bringing them together in the democracy of a common cause in the collegiate life. In the autumn, when the candidates for the team are being tried out and selected according to their worth, thousands of healthy young men take their places on the athletic field every afternoon. These hours in the open air are spent in beneficial exercise and, even if the candidate does not succeed in making the team, he is storing up for himself a fund of health from which to draw in later years. Besides, to a candidate disappointed in making the 'Varsity team, or the second eleven, there are positions waiting on the class teams.

One of the most impressive structures in the country is the Harvard stadium. Massive in construction, with a seating capacity of over 35,000, contributed by a class which has long since left the immediate influences of the institution, it is built essentially for the future and for football. Long after many of the buildings now used for the dissemination of learning at Cambridge have been replaced by newer edifices, the Harvard stadium will stand, impressive and entire, a monument to energetic manhood illustrated in football, and will ring with shouts and songs as rival colleges meet in contests of skill and strength in years to come.

Throughout the country, at the different universities, have been and are being erected structures intended for the same purpose. They are being built with a view to the permanency of the game to which they are adapted. These edifices are being erected at an enormous expense, it is true, with a view to the future, but are nevertheless necessary to meet the present demands of those who desire to witness the playing of the scheduled games of each season.

Wherever the game is being played—and this scope is limited only by the presence of schools and colleges, for these institutions are practically unanimous in their support of football—representative people of that particular section are attracted by football contests as by no other athletic event of the year. If football answered no other purpose than that of drawing the hundreds of thousands into the open air, away from offices and shops, drawing rooms and clubs, for a few health-giving hours, this would be reason enough for its existence.

Anyone who can be present as a spectator at one of the big football games of the year and can look on without enthusiasm as the game progresses is lacking in red blood and can expect no pleasure in outdoor sport. Football has earned for itself a unique place in the life of this country and deserves the position it has acquired. It is the national autumn sport, without a rival, and as such will retain its position as long as Anglo-Saxon blood flows in the veins of the young American.

No better evidence is found of the popularity which football has attained and the natural attractiveness and benefit which it brings, than the rapidity with which the game has swept over the preparatory and high schools of the country. From the colleges, the original homes of football, have gone out each year football players who have adopted teaching as their life work. These men have carried into their new positions a knowledge of the game which has been eagerly received wherever they have gone. Every preparatory school now has one or more instructors, a regular portion of whose labors is the instruction of the pupils of the school, in football, and the development of a team which shall properly represent the school on the gridiron. By this method the game has gained myriads of friends and adherents who in their college and university courses keep up their devotion to football. It also develops the young players along the correct lines and moulds the play of the schoolboys in ways which not only benefit the player, but develop him for the more important contests that will come when he reaches his chosen school of higher learning.

The necessity for an adequate field on which the game may be played in the high and preparatory schools has generally arisen all over the country and often the popularity of the game from the spectator's standpoint has provided the means of equipping the field and paying the expense. Some preparatory schools are far better off than many colleges in this respect and many of them maintain a football field and equipment complete in every particular. It is true that ideals are not always carried out and that the game and its influence are not always for the best. This is true of practically everything in life.

The photographic reproductions accompanying this

Marshall Field, Chicago—Chicago vs. Illinois.   *Photo by Geo. R. Lawrence.*

chapter portray better than is possible by words the great concourse of people regularly attracted to the big football games all over the country. Such crowds, while largely composed of college people, could not be gathered from these alone. The spectators at a football match come from all walks of life and include thousands who love the game solely as a spectacle and an exhibition of concerted pluck and action. There is no crowd so cosmopolitan as that at a football game and this is, after all the most effective testimonial to the hold the game has, east, west, north and south, on the hearts of the American public.

FOOTBALL

WHAT IT DOES FOR THE PLAYER PHYSICALLY, MEN-
TALLY AND MORALLY

No American game has won so much praise and, at the same time, so much censure, as has football. The game has been lauded for the scientific play it develops and for the training of mind and body it affords the players. It has been adversely criticised for its roughness and the consequent injuries which the players are likely to receive. From the point of view of some spectators the game seems so dangerous to the players that to allow the game to be played in our colleges seems half-civilized.

Such persons are not really well acquainted with football as it is played today for the game is first in the many forms of athletic competition in the development of the player physically, mentally and morally.

Although to the layman football is primarily a physical game, the bodily benefits afforded the player are by no means the only ones he receives. True, it does afford the player better opportunities for physical development than any other sport. In most other branches of competitive athletics only parts of the body are brought into exercise. In football all muscles are used alike. The arms, legs and back are all required to do their work. The running and swift succession of plays develop the endurance. In every possible way the muscles of the player are hardened. Furthermore, no single part of him is developed abnormally. Football players do not become slow, muscle-bound men. They develop into smooth, enduring athletes. The physical development derived from football is readily shown by the charts of college trainers, giving the physical measurements of football players before and after they have become veterans. In every case the measurements show a remarkable growth in strength, size and symmetry for the athlete.

The physical benefits, while generally admitted, have often been counted of little value, however, because of the roughness of a game which, it has been claimed, injures more players than it benefits.

That football is brutal, no one who is acquainted with the game will admit. All will concede that the game is rough but roughness does not constitute brutality. Liability to injury on the part of the players cannot be entirely eliminated but this is true of every game and occupation in life. In almost every town where football is played it will be found that such sports as boating, hunting, skating and the rest furnish more serious accidents each year than does the game of football. Since our whole lives are made up of physical risks, any game which has no element whatever of roughness or risk is hardly worthy of young and vigorous men.

However, the roughness of football should be eliminated as much as possible and this is done to a great extent among our great teams today. These teams are trained by skilled men whose sole duty it is to see that each player is fit to do his part in the game. Furthermore, the players are usually taught the principles of gentlemanly conduct and much of the roughness of the game is eliminated in this way. Football is being made more and more a game of physical and mental skill, rather than a contest of mere force. The old style of mass plays is giving way to the more scientific and open variety. All this tends to eliminate the liability of serious injury to the player and at the same time affords him the very best opportunity for physical development.

Princeton Field—Yale vs. Princeton.

Photo by Barr McIntosh.

But the physical benefits of football are of no greater importance to the average college man than are its advantages to his mental development. Football is a game of strength, but of strength properly controlled by the mind. Many games are won by the mental superiority of one team over another. This is a phase of football with which the average spectator is entirely unfamiliar. He can easily see the push and scramble on the field but he cannot comprehend the workings of the minds that direct the efforts of both sides. However, any spectator ought to be able to appreciate the severe mental drill given to the player when, in order to be successful, he must learn a mass of rules and be able to understand them all and act accordingly; master a system of signals and carry them out instantly; understand his own play and that of his fellows so that they all work together with the precision of a machine, and do all this with a quickness and accuracy demanded by no other game.

It is very evident that a dullard can never play football properly. Hence it is by no means detrimental to the game to require high standings for all football men in their class room work, as is the case in most colleges. Almost all the football players who have attained any recognized degree of success are good students. Football not only requires keen-minded men to play it but it makes its players still keener of mind. The regular exercise helps the player and makes his head clearer for study. It makes him quick in thought and able to grasp things with precision. Further, football, by bringing the player into contact with many opponents whom he must watch very carefully and shrewdly, is sure to develop his ability to read character. This is a very important benefit, often overlooked.

Along with the mental benefits of football comes the

moral development, of which the most evident characteristic is courage. Every manly man must have a certain amount of courage, physical and mental, and no football player can long be without it. It requires a great deal of mental bravery to run into a foreseen possible physical danger as all players must often do. Then, mental courage is developed in the player in several distinct ways. Every player must learn to have perfect control of his temper, so that he may always play with discretion and never disgrace himself or his school by forgetting what the etiquette of the gridiron demands. A player must learn to be calm and rational in the most exciting moments, for it is at such times that the most is expected of him. He must never get "rattled" but must use his head all the time. Further, a great amount of self-control and self-denial must be exercised by the ordinary young college man when he begins training. He must yield himself readily to authority and must learn to obey both quickly and quietly.

Obedience must be exercised not only on the field but also off the gridiron, for it is in the latter place that its sway calls for the most will power. Here the player must obey the rule of regular rising and retiring and must learn never to break it, no matter what temptations he may have. The player must also exercise great control in sticking to the diet assigned him. He must never yield to the possible temptations to drink or smoke, but must accustom himself to regular habits regarding his daily nourishment. All these influences toward self-control are very important for college men and, as football brings them all to bear in the fall of the year when many of the players are away from home for the first time, the moral effects of the game cannot be overestimated.

It is true, of course, that there are exceptions to the

rule in the general results of football. Instincts are developed in some players which do not redound to their advantage in after life. Injuries are possible in all sports as in the daily avocations. There are lawyers whose careers turn out anything but an ornament to the great profession and cases can be cited of clergymen who have disgraced their cloth, yet in neither instance is there a possible stigma to be cast on their co-workers who are sincerely benefiting the world by the same knowledge acquired by those who have perverted it. All football players do not come out of the great game unscathed physically or morally, yet the great majority who do achieve benefit from it, and marked benefit too, amply demonstrate the value of the game as a source of all-round development.

Football is undoubtedly the best American game, not only from the average spectator's point of view, but from that of the player as well.

The many and conflicting opinions regarding the effect of football on the players, not only in college but after graduation and judged from both the physical and mental points of view, led a prominent Bostonian to ask the Harvard Board of Overseers for an investigation. No formal defense of football has been attempted, in spite of repeated assaults on the game by sensational newspaper and magazine writers.

Mr. Robert Bacon, of the board to whom the matter was referred, came to New Haven and solicited successfully the services of Mr. Walter Camp, the best known authority on the game and a veteran player himself, to act as the chairman of a committee which should thoroughly investigate the matter. Mr. Camp accepted and, with the assistance of Rev. Joseph Twitchell of Hartford, Conn., a member of the Yale corporation; Rev. Endicott Peabody

of Groton school, Mass.; James W. Alexander of Princeton, and Hon. Henry E. Howland of New York, Messrs.
Camp and Bacon took up the work of amassing the facts.

A thorough canvass was made of the veteran football
players of Harvard, Yale and Princeton and a mass of testimony was secured from team captains, college authorities,
preparatory school masters, and the result was a most complete array of data, proving beyond a doubt that football
is a game in which the beneficent effects far outnumber the
possible drawbacks.

Without going into the detail which is presented in such
a wealth of array in Mr. Camp's "Facts and Figures," a
work which finds its subject matter in the results of the investigation, the committee's findings may well be summarized in a few paragraphs of their report, which includes the
following:

"We find that the almost unanimous opinion of those
who have played the game of football at Harvard, Yale or
Princeton during the last eighteen years is that it has been
of marked benefit to them, both in the way of general development and mental discipline; also that they regard the
injuries sustained as generally unimportant and far out-
weighed by the benefits. Still further similar enquiries sent
out to the players of the majority of college teams have
brought back the same unvarying replies, testifying that
the game was of great benefit to the player both mentally
and physically.

"While it was fair to conclude that men who had been
out of college all the way from two or three years to six-
teen or seventeen would be fully competent to judge of the
effects of the game upon themselves, it seemed that something more would be necessary in the case of the schoolboy
who had not yet entered college. For this reason our en-

quiries were made not only of the boy himself but of the teacher as well. The head masters also of most of the prominent schools were courteous enough to reply quite at length to our request for an expression of opinion. We find that the evidence here too, is that, in the majority of cases, the sport has been beneficial to the physical development and discipline of the school and that the consensus of opinion is that scholarship has certainly not suffered."

The summarized statistics collected by the committee from the Harvard, Yale and Princeton students is as follows:

Number of men who considered themselves benefited, 328; number of men who considered themselves injured, 3; number of men who failed to reply, 2; number of men who considered it had no effect, 4.

Substantially the same ratio applied to the same questions, asked in reference to the effect of the game on the player's mental equipment.

FOOTBALL

FROM THE SPECTATOR'S POINT OF VIEW

Football the spectacle—where in athletic competitions, ancient, mediaeval or modern do you find its equal? The ease with which the general principle of the game is comprehended by the spectator, the facility afforded for every individual of the thousands assembled to see every play, the contagious enthusiasm that sweeps the most blasé into the fever of excitement that is prevalent on every side—all combine to make the struggle on the gridiron one of absorbing interest.

Let us join the multitude that annually flocks to the scene of one of the contests which form the closing and most important features of a football season.

It is a bright November day, warm enough for comfort in the sunshine but sufficiently crisp to tell us that we should be well wrapped up for the two hours, more or less, that we are to spend on the field. We mingle in the crowd of undergraduates, alumni, invited friends of the students and other devotees of football who are wending their way to the athletic field. Many of them have traveled hundreds of miles to be present today. Some of them are "Old Grads" who, heroes of the gridiron battles of former years, are back at the scene of their old triumphs and disappointments for the big athletic event of the year. Members of the faculty are in the throng. A carriage passes, bearing the venerable president of the University. In a compact body are moving a regiment of students from the visiting university which is the foe today. They flaunt their colors, and their songs alternate with their college cheer. Towns-

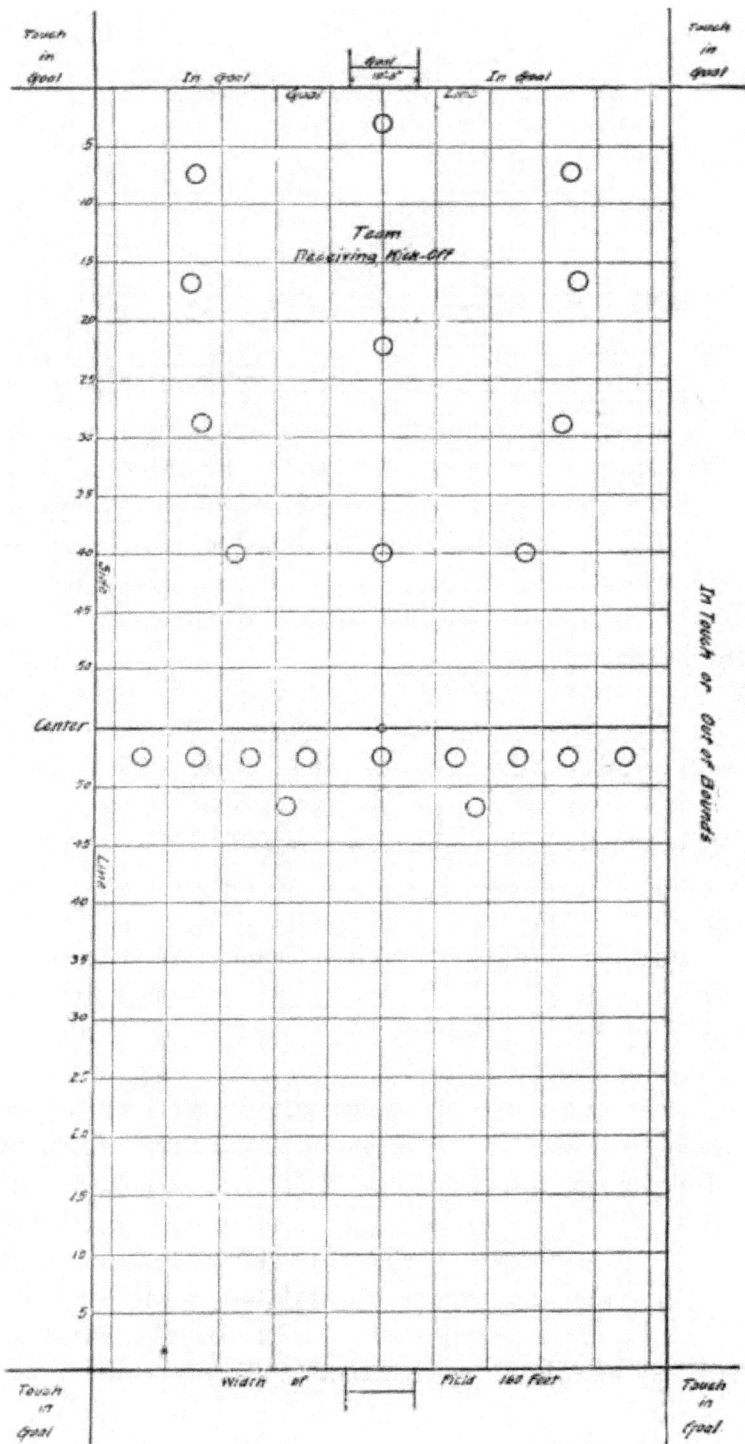

Touch in Goal   In Goal   Goal 18.5°   In Goal   Touch in Goal

Goal   Line

Team
Receiving Kick-Off

Side

Line

Center

In Touch or Out of Bounds

Touch in Goal   Width of   Field 160 Feet   Touch in Goal

DIAGRAM OF FIELD—TEAMS LINED UP FOR KICK-OFF.

people, excursionists, sportsmen of all sorts—they are all
going to see the game.

Our seats have been selected weeks ago, so there is no
occasion to take part in the hurly-burly that attends the acquisition of a place in the general admission stands, for a
good view of the game is indispensable. We soon make
our way to our places, the sun at our backs, the field sweeping down past us, fifty-five yards on either side.

Although it is still a half-hour before the game will begin, the crowd is already here. The gridiron—for the old
name still sticks to the field of play in spite of its present
checker-board form—is resplendent in its glaring lines of
white, the center of an amphitheatre that seems a continuous bank of people from end to end and from side to
side. To the left and right of us and across the ends of
the field—everywhere but in that one section directly across
from us—gleam the colors of the school whose supporters
we are. Over there though, dark against the lighter sur-
roundings, stand out the flags and streamers of the supporters of the visiting team. Outnumbered hopelessly
when it comes to a show of vocal enthusiasm, they have
gathered together and their cheer, clean cut and following
to perfection every movement of the cane of their yell-
master, sounds a plucky defiance to the flood of sound that
is regularly evoked by the batons of the leaders of the home
school who are distributed along our front.

Song follows song, some the music of the old epics
of the school, handed down for many years, some of it
verses especially manufactured for the occasion by the
student bards, and practiced until letter- if not note-perfect
at many a mass meeting.

A gate opens at the farther end of the grounds, there is
a vociferous cheer from the nearest section and the team

in whose success our hopes are centered, trots out on the field, to be met by a tumult of welcome. Big fellows they are, stout of limb and victors through the season over every team they have met. From the other entrance to the grid-iron the visitors enter and they seem every bit as strong and fit to maintain the undefeated record which they also boast this year. Footballs are produced, the two teams form in large circles in different parts of the field and begin to toss the ovals about in rapid succession, while the enthusiasts in stands and bleachers cheer their heroes till it seems as if their throats would be insufficient for the strain which one or the other side, if not both, will have to bear through the game that is not yet begun.

From each team a man detaches himself and, with a man in citizens' clothes, looks over the field. He is the captain and his companion is the coach. He tests the consistency of the surface of the field, notes the direction of the wind, the effects of the sunshine and the other conditions which, if properly observed, will give one side an advantage over the other at some stage in the progress of the game. A couple of wet spots are carefully noted, for in a close game these things may mean victory or defeat. There is a fresh breeze from the west and this makes it practically certain that the west goal will be selected by the captain who wins the toss. The effect of the opening rush is most important, for it is a remarkable team that can summon enough reserve power to win a game after having been played off its feet in the opening half. Later in the day, too, the wind will probably lighten, so the advantage will be less important then.

But look! The captains rejoin their teams, the elevens line up in battle array, a signal is called by each of the quarter backs and the lines charge down the field, each

practicing the plays that are to be relied on today to bring
victory.

Observe, my friend, these twenty-two young men who
are to do their best for their schools in the game today.
It is no small honor for a man to be selected for duty
at such a time as this. Some of them have been denying
themselves the creature comforts of life for years, under-
going training that the Spartan of ancient times might
have gloried in, just for this chance. In this throng are
friends, brothers, sisters—yes sweethearts—who have eyes
for but one out there on the field. They trust him today.
He knows it and, glorying in his strength, is determined
to do or die in this game which is upon us. Over there on
that bench where the substitutes sit there are many sore
hearts this day, for, when a man is selected to play one of
those eleven positions, a full half-dozen are downcast in
disappointment.

But the game must soon be started. The signal practice
changes a bit and each side passes the ball to its chosen
kicker, to allow him a final test of his ability. The captains toss the coin for the choice of goals and the visitors
win. The whistle of the referee calls the teams into
position and the contest is on.

From now on till this game is finished, each of the
twenty-two young men out there will have but one ambition—the transportation of the ball across the enemy's
goal line. The objective point of our own team is the final
white line over there to the left, while the enemy's eleven
will strive in the opposite direction. Each man on each
team will have a part to perform, whether it be the carrying
of the ball himself or assisting his comrades, and unless each man does that part his team will fail in its attempts. There is one main way in which the ball is legally

FRANKLIN FIELD, PENNSYLVANIA—Army vs. Navy.

advanced. This is in the arms of a runner. Passed from
hand to hand it may be, and each scrimmage necessarily
starts that way, but the passes must never be made in the
direction of the opponents' goal. As a last resort the ball
may be kicked forward but this, as a rule, only when progress by the regular plan seems impossible. In but two
other ways can points be scored: One when a team is able
to propel the ball by drop-kicks or by a kick from placement above that bar at the center of the goal line and between the posts which form a capital H at each end; the
other method being when one side voluntarily touches the
ball down behind its own goal. This is termed a safety
and counts two points for the opponents. It is but rarely
seen, however, in the big games.

Squarely in front of us forms our team, stretching across
the field along the 55-yard line which marks the middle.
In the exact center the ball is carefully stood on end, ready
for the kick-off, which is the method of putting it in play.
Defending the west goal the visiting team, which has won
the choice of positions, is so disposed in scattered array
over the half of the field that the kick which is coming, regardless of its direction, may fall into the ready arms of
some waiting player.

Once more the referee's whistle blows. In front of us
the line charges forward and in its middle the kicker meets
the ball with the swing of his foot and sends it high in air,
straight for the enemy's goal posts.

The full back of the visiting team stands under the goal,
arms outstretched. A half-dozen of the others form in
front of him. He catches the ball and sprints up the field
in the middle of that solid phalanx, running it back. For
15 yards the formation pursues an uninterrupted course.
Then one of our tackles plunges low into the interference,

the first obstacle which it has met. He is trampled under foot, but another man follows, and then four or five more. The phalanx is broken, but out behind circles the runner, now relying on his own efforts to make the gain longer. From the side darts in one of our ends, launching himself at the runner's knees. The man with the ball tries to dodge but it is too late. Down they go together. The play is stopped.

The referee's whistle blows again and the visitors line up with the ball in their possession. The name of the tackler is cheered from ten thousand throats.

The teams are now playing on the 25-yard line of the visitors. To score against us, the ball must be carried to the opposite end of the field, across the goal line of the home eleven, or else cleverly kicked by drop or placement, between our goal posts. It is a long distance to be gained but there is plenty of time to accomplish the feat if the enemy's eleven has the grit and power to do it.

Watch the referee. He is the official who has charge of the ball and who, assisted by the linesmen who do the measuring, decides whether it has been legally advanced or not and how far. On the opposite end of the line is the umpire. He is the one who notes the actions of the men in each play, guarding against any infraction of the rules which prescribe in detail the lawful ways in which each of these young giants may use his strength, for the play must be clean and the interpretation of the rules is always strict.

You will now see the use of the chalk lines which, five yards apart, cross the entire field. The visitors have no right to maintain possession of the ball if in three trials they fail to carry it at least the five yards intervening between two of these lines. Failing to do this, they will afford our young heroes their opportunity.

Only less important are the lines which divide the field longitudinally. Also five yards apart, these lines assist the officials in limiting the play to strict observance of the rule which makes it obligatory for runners receiving the ball on direct pass from the center to circle at least five yards before progressing toward the opponents' goal.

Note the way the men line up for the scrimmage, the visitors in offensive array—for they have the ball—our men on defense, the line of battle being in each case the one which, with a few variations, has proven the best in the judgment of the men who have made the game a life study.

The centers, as their names imply, are the center men of each line. On either side of them are the guards and outside these, the tackles. The men on the extremities of each line are, quite logically, the ends. The side with the ball, you will note, however, has drawn its ends close in to the general formation, while ours are ranging wide. The men playing the positions mentioned comprise what is technically known as the line, differentiating them from the other four members of the eleven, who are termed backs. The quarter back is the man immediately behind the center. On offense, when his side is carrying the ball, he calls the signals which tell the players of a team, in a language which they alone understand, the play to be employed, the man who will carry the ball and the direction in which he is to carry it. The quarter, when ready, takes the ball from his center, who passes it back between his legs, and, in turn, passes it on again, always backward— for a forward pass is illegal—to the back who is selected to carry it into the enemy's country. The rest assist the runner in the manner in which they have been taught. Frequently in the progress of a game a member of the line is called back to relieve the backs in carrying the ball and

RANDALL FIELD, WISCONSIN.—Minnesota vs. Wisconsin.

their linesmen block opponents out of their way on offense, while the defensive line endeavors to stop the play. On the defense, half backs take the places ours have now—back of the tackles to assist the ends, for this is a frequent point of attack. The full back of the attacking side stands directly behind the quarter, with the halves on either side of him, while our full back is 30 yards or so behind his own line, waiting for a possible punt and acting as a final line of defense, should the opposing runner succeed in carrying the ball past the rest of his comrades.

The location of the ball forms an imaginary line between the teams, across which no player may charge till the oval is snapped by the center.

But watch! The enemy's quarter has called his signal, the ball is snapped back by the center and the left half back, who takes the ball from the quarter, surrounded by the other backs there to protect him from tacklers, charges obliquely across and into our left tackle. Our own half rushes forward to meet the interference and dives into it. Circling around behind the mêlée, which has now been charged by our left tackle also, the runner with the ball emerges all alone and turns toward our goal. Our end closes in, leaps for the runner's knees and throws him fiercely to the ground. The whistle again and the referee calls out, "Second down, three yards to gain." The foe has traveled two yards of that long trip toward our goal.

Again the signals, again the passing, again the rush, but this time it is the enemy's full back who takes the ball. He plunges straight ahead for our center as if the line of men before him had no existence. Between our center and one of the guards, the runner's line men have made a big hole and through it dashes the man with the ball, to fall into the arms of our quarter back, whom he drags a short distance before being downed.

"First down, five yards to gain," again sings out the referee. The rush has netted the requisite distance without the third attempt and the foe can now begin all over again. On all sides of us the home team is adjured to "Hold them," while from the hostile camp across the gridiron rings out a stentorian cheer for the man who made the gain and the school for which he made it.

Again the full back assaults our center, but this time, with a thud of human bone and muscle, plainly audible where we sit, he is stopped as solidly as if it had been a brick wall instead of a human rampart which he was battering with his head and shoulders. Again the human missile is launched at our center and again the gallant fellow stops the play, although the runner manages to wiggle a scant yard while he is falling.

Once more rings out the signal. The foe's formation suddenly changes. The backs form a wedge with the full back, ten yards back of the center, at the open end. It is the formation for a punt, the kick productive of the greatest possible distance and the inevitable result when a team fails to gain by carrying the ball. Another futile attempt at the ends or the line would have handed over possession of the ball to our team with but 30 yards to travel to a touchdown, and this would have been poor generalship.

Back from the center comes the ball as the kicker holds out his hands and on that instant our men charge. The ball, dropped from his hands and meeting the kicker's foot just before it reaches the ground, is booted high in air and down the field. Under it scurries our own full back, 50 yards behind his own line, while his comrades in front of him are doing their best to keep the opponents from getting through in time to make a tackle far down the field. The catch is beautifully executed and the runner starts sprint-

ing back. One of the enemy's ends does succeed in getting
through, however, and rushes to meet him. The full back
dodges, eludes him and comes tearing up the field while,
all about us, men are urging him on. Friend and foe now
mingle alike before him, one helping him, another endeavoring to bring him down. Full 30 yards he comes and then,
dodging one tackler, rushes right into the arms of another.
It is our ball and our turn to carry the oval.

But that visiting team has a defense that is every bit as
strong as its supporters have told us. Twice our plays are
thrown back and it becomes the duty of our quarter to call
for a kick, as theirs did a few minutes ago. The punt sails
high in air, although not so far as the effort of the opposing full back, who has the assistance of the wind. The
oval twists deceptively and seems to travel a spiral course.
The man in the enemy's backfield, there to catch it, runs
in, stretches out his arms, misjudges a bit and the ball
strikes him, falls, takes a bound to the side and rolls away.

"A fumble," shriek ten thousand throats. Like a shot,
through the rush of men one of our ends tears in, dives for
the ball, rolling over and over. He grasps it in both arms
and tries to regain his feet for a run to the opponents' goal,
but there is a man who throws himself at him and flattens
him to earth again. It is our ball, however, but 15 yards
from the goal, and a touchdown almost within our grasp.
Can the team make it?

Almost before the enemy's eleven has recovered from
the consternation into which the fumble has thrown it, our
men sweep them off their feet again. Straight through the
center tears our full back for six yards on the first down.
Our left half turns three yards more around their end. We
have them "on the run" and our wise little captain knows it.
Through the line the full back again plows his furrow, and

PERCY FIELD, CORNELL.—Princeton vs. Cornell.

Photo by Burr McIntosh.

when he is stopped there is but a yard left to go. Once more the full back is called on but this time the desperate foe is waiting for him and he fails. An attempt at an end run is also thrown back by our plucky foe. It is do or die this time. There is a feint of two or three men at one end, the enemy's defense is drawn away from the center, and once more the full back, with but two men helping him this time, assaults this position.

The play is in plain sight of every spectator except those directly in front of it. Thousands of people give a mighty shove as if to help the runner. He goes through, he keeps going. He falls over the line. It is a touchdown, the regular method of scoring, and the scene in the stands and bleachers beggars description. The undergraduates cheer and do it in defiance of the yell masters who vainly try to infuse into the demonstration some of the system which has been so prominent up to this time. Women shriek, men of middle age throw their hats high in air and forget what directions the headgear take. It is simply pandemonium.

But the referee pulls off the men, and our captain, with a chosen player, accurate in kicking ability, walks out in direct line with where the ball was carried across the goal line. The touchdown has scored us five points. If a goal can be secured by a place-kick, one more point will be added. About 25 yards from the line, almost in front of the goal, the little captain stretches himself prostrate, holding the ball at arm's length a scant inch above the ground. The opponents line up on their goal line. The kicker measures his distance. With an almost imperceptible motion the ball is lowered to the ground, the foot meets it and the opposing ranks rush forward to block the kick. Squarely over the bar and between the posts sails the ball. The score is 6 to 0.

But there is no rest for the players and, having changed goals, they speedily line up for another kick-off. This time it is the opponents who have the chance to start the play, and our men scatter themselves over their half of the field to handle the kick-off. The kick is made and caught and the runner is downed.

The pride of the home university again carry the ball toward the opponents' goal.

But this time the entire length of the field stretches out before them. These visitors have gotten over their panic and are playing the game. A punt is necessary at our 35-yard line and the enemy's little quarter catches truly and circles wide. Watch him, for he is fleet of foot and a famous dodger. One of our ends makes a dive for him with outstretched arms, but grasps nothing but empty air. Clear back to the line of scrimmage he twists, dodges and runs through that open field. From far down near his own goal our full back rushes to intercept him. It is the last chance for a tackle. Right down the edge of the field tears the runner with the ball. There is no room to dodge this time without carrying the ball out of bounds. A clutch follows the dive and the man with the ball rolls over the sideline, stopped, but only after a 40-yard run that is destined to be chronicled as the feature play of the game.

If you are an old habitué of the football bleachers, my friend, you have found a moment in which to take your glance away from that flying runner to the section across the field where his friends are herded, comparatively quiet through all the play that has come before. The glance is well worth the reward. The moments while that runner was tearing down the field were sweet ones over there. Still as the Pacific on a calm day, the dark-hued banners had rested, streamers down, through the gloom that had preceded. The change is something wonderful. A volcano suddenly sprung into activity could not seeth or roar like that. It is their first chance and how they are making the most of it. But we return their cheer for their runner, with one for the man who made the tackle and saved an almost certain touchdown, then settling our eyes on the visitors' eleven to see what they will do now within striking distance of our goal.

Thirty yards from our goal line the visitors walk back into the field, the referee pacing off 15 yards toward the middle where the teams line up again. Can we hold them?

A half back rushes straight for our goal from his position on the side nearer the center of the field, but is thrown for a gain so slight as to be practically nothing. A wide circling run places the ball squarely in mid-field but no closer to the goal line. It is the third down and the cheers for the plucky defense are deafening. They cannot rush our line; so much is certain, yet there is something else which they may accomplish.

The enemy forms for a drop kick. Back from the center comes the ball, squarely into the hands of the full back, well behind his line. Clear to the ground in front of him the kicker drops the ball, as he swings his foot, while our warriors charge through in a vain endeavor to block the kick. The ball strikes the ground, the foot meets it with a steady swing and the oval rises high, spinning like a top. On it floats, perfectly in line with its desired course. It clears the bar with a foot or two to spare and again the visitors split their throats, while the thousands about us are silent. It has scored four points for the enemy, but we are still ahead, and our captain brings the ball out to the center of the field, there to be kicked off again.

Had the kick missed, a touchback would have resulted, which would have entitled the home team to the ball. It

West Point Field, Parade Grounds—West Point vs. Yale.   Photo by Burr McIntosh.

would then have been brought out 25 yards and there kicked again, but back toward the enemy's goal, in order to place it in play again.

It is a great game, and the remainder of the 35 minutes in the first half—for the teams are playing the full length of time allowed by the rules—sees neither team gaining a perceptible advantage, although the school for whose victory the majority of the big crowd is praying is undoubtedly the better on the line of scrimmage. The presence of so fine a kicker on the enemy's eleven makes the contest still doubtful, although he will have to sacrifice some of his accuracy and distance in the half that is coming on account of the change in goals, which will make it necessary for him to kick against the wind.

It is plainly evident in the opening minutes of the second half, after the ten-minute rest is over, that our captain believes he has discovered the enemy's real weakness. Right tackle seems the destination of more than half the plays which our men start, and they gain steadily. From the kick-off the ball is taken straight up the field, the backs handling the oval cleanly and the interference being well nigh perfect. The tackle who is bearing the brunt of the terrific attack lies prostrate on the ground after every play and is plainly weakening under the human bombardment. On his own 30-yard line the visitors' captain calls a halt. With tears in his eyes and sobbing like a little child, the unfortunate tackle wraps a blanket about him and is guided off the field, while a substitute, wild with joy at his chance, rushes in to take his place.

But the recruit is the possessor of a zeal that is dangerous. Before our center snaps the ball the new tackle charges and meets the ball behind our line. He tackles the runner and throws him for a loss, but the eagle eye of the umpire has seen the infraction of the rules, for no player of either side may cross the scrimmage line before the ball is snapped. The umpire takes the ball in hand and paces off five yards toward the enemy's goal, giving us the ball again. The off-side play was a costly one.

Steadily we approach their goal line once more and their defense, while futile, increases in desperation. Our full back plunges through the line and emerges squarely in front of the defensive quarter. The visitor forgets himself in the frenzy of defeat that seems certain, and his clenched fist shoots home. The blow was covertly given but the umpire is there to see such things. There is another distance penalty and the young man guilty of the slugging is sent from the game, while both sides cheer the decision. Foul play has no part in clean football.

With the further weakening of the visiting eleven there is no chance for them longer to hope to win the game. Over and through them the plays travel regularly. Every formation plunges into the line. Our resourceful captain's plan of attack is just versatile enough to prevent anticipation, while still maintaining a uniformity that invariably yields results. From two to four yards and even more are gained on almost every down. Still the bombardment of that line with those missiles of human brawn continues.

The enemy's ends keep drawing closer to the main body, to relieve their harassed comrades. Suddenly that close formation in which our backs have been playing melts into a thin line that charges widely around in a sweeping circle. The little quarter back takes the ball from the center and this time hugs it to his own breast, scudding along without passing it. It is the direct pass run and it has been signalled at just the proper moment. Behind his flying rampart the quarter back speeds safely along. His interference carries him past everybody but the opposing full back, for the play has caught the enemy's ends out of their places. It is a tackle or a touchdown now, for this is the last line of defense.

The full back leaps forward to make the tackle and just as he plunges, the runner rises in air as if to leap an obstruction. The tackler is cleanly cleared in a spectacular manner and, with the cheers of the thousands deafening his ears, the runner crosses the line for a touchdown and five points more, after a thrilling run.

But the goal line was crossed far from the posts which mark the middle and an attempt to kick goal from the angle which results along such a perpendicular would be hazardous. Accordingly a punt-out is decided on.

In front of the goal and 10 to 20 yards from it, a half-dozen of our men line up, while the full back stands, the ball in hand, right where the runner crossed the goal line. The full back punts the ball right into the midst of his comrades and the enemy charges, but all too late. One of the half backs has caught the punt and heeled it, making the place kick possible. The added point from the goal kick which follows is easily secured.

With the score 12 to 4 in our favor it seems certain that the game cannot now result in a defeat in the 15 minutes that remain to be played.

The side whose goal line has been crossed has the kick-off, of course. Again we start our march toward their goal, far up the field. It is still a fight, every inch of it, but the visitors are playing now solely to save the name of their Alma Mater from disgrace. Defeat is certain, but the spirit of the team inspires its men to keep playing the game with a zeal that cannot but rouse our admiration. Occasionally their brace gives them possession of the ball and once their

feared, fleet runner brings back a punt for a thrilling dash of 30 yards, but he cannot play the whole game alone to a successful conclusion.

Forgetful of the sting of defeat which may be ours some day, the great crowd still cheers every play. From across the field a loyal encouragement is still given by the visitors to their beaten team. The hopes of months are going down to defeat, but the men who are beaten have done their best and, when the final whistle is blown and the game is over, the players of each team gather close together and cheer each other after the style of true sportsmen who have tested each others' mettle with mutual respect.

Let us start homeward. It is time for us to prepare for the festivities of the evening. There will be lively times around the old campus tonight.

FOOTBALL

ITS VARIED CHARACTERISTICS AS PLAYED IN THE DIFFERENT PARTS OF THE UNITED STATES

PRINCETON

Princeton is one of the schools in which football found its origin in the United States, and the game has been played there on a systematic basis ever since 1876, when relations were established with Yale. In the following year a similar agreement was entered into with Harvard and continued until 1897.

Among the football stars developed at Princeton are Cowan, Poe, Ames, Wheeler, King, Trenchard, Lea, Church, Kelly, Cochran, Hillebrand and Edwards.

Most faithfully throughout the history of football has Princeton maintained the strictly regular system of play. All the offensive operations are directed with seven men in the line and rarely is the ball entrusted to any member of the team not a regular occupant of the backfield. This gives a much less varied style of attack and is a consequent deterrent to success, beyond a doubt, but the wonderful spirit which has been the possession of every Princeton team has assisted its successive elevens to maintain a high place in the athletic world, nevertheless.

The Princeton defense places the ends rather wide, the tackles similarly free and the three backs supporting the line.

The Princeton style of game is generally the most freely imitated all over the United States. This is partially on account of its simplicity and partially on account of the large number of Princeton graduates who have taken up football coaching after leaving college.

PRINCETON OFFENSE—Mass on Tackle.

MICHIGAN

The University of Michigan is one of the oldest western schools in point of football experience. Her most universal rival has been Chicago, although relations have long
been maintained with Wisconsin and intermittently with
Minnesota.

Such players as Baird, Ferbert, Henninger, Senter,
Bloomingston, Bennett, Widman, McLean, Weeks, Snow,
McGugin, Herrnstein and Heston have left bright records
on the football tablets of the "Wolverines."

Coached in past years by graduates of several styles of
play, Michigan has been since 1901 under the tutelage of
F. H. Yost, under whom has been developed an offense
generally described as shifting, men being drawn back frequently from the line for the purpose of attack. The ends
are also frequently drawn into the backfield, their places
being taken by the backs. A shifting interference, in which
the point of attack is veiled, is also a feature of the Michigan play.

On defense the Michigan teams adapt their tactics to
best meet the attack of their opponents, sometimes leaving
three men in the secondary line of defense, sometimes two.
Generally considered, it might be termed shifting, like the
offense.

HARVARD

Football has been played at Harvard University since the earliest days of the game in the United States. Mutual relations with Yale were established in 1876 and have been maintained up to the present. Annual games were played with Princeton from 1877 to 1897. Harvard and Pennsylvania have maintained their mutual rivalry almost continuously since 1881.

The annals of Harvard football redound with the names of such players as Comstock, Dean, Newell, Waters, Lewis, Wrightington, Dibblee and Daly, all of whom are among the greatest players the game has ever known.

In the offensive system of play in vogue at Harvard, the "tandem" is the most prominent. This formation is usually made up of the three backs, although sometimes one of the linemen is called back for use in the play, the back left out of the formation taking the place of the lineman in the latter's regular position. The tackle-back play has also been a feature of Harvard's attack until very recently.

The Harvard defense is what may be termed regular, although the ends play in close to tackle.

Graduate coaching has been the rule at Harvard and the result has been a maintenance of old football styles and traditions which have been little varied in the passing of the years.

HARVARD ON THE OFFENSE, PENNSYLVANIA ON THE DEFENSE.

MINNESOTA

The football team of the University of Minnesota has long held a high position among the other western teams, athletic relations of an intermittent character having been maintained with Illinois, Northwestern, Chicago and Michigan, and a regular series having been played with the University of Wisconsin eleven.

Among the players who have been prominent as stars at Minnesota are Harding, Pillsbury, Flynn, Schacht, Rogers, Thorpe, Van Valkenburg, Strathearn, Knowlton and Irsfield.

Coached by Dr. H. L. Williams, the former Yale half back and hurdler, the elevens of Minnesota have developed strongly along the Yale lines of play, to which has been added, however, a series of line shifts and tackle-back plays combined, making an attack frequently after the fashion of a wing shift. As a rule the regular defensive formations are maintained.

While the comparative geographical isolation of Minnesota's location has tended to make the securing of games with the other large western schools a matter of difficulty, there is no institution east or west in which there is a more enthusiastic support offered to its team than is afforded annually at Minnesota.

YALE

Football has been played at Yale since 1876, when mutual relations were established with Harvard and Princeton which have continued practically without interruption ever since. Yale also played a game with the University of Pennsylvania team in each season from 1879 to 1894 inclusive.

Prominent places in Yale football history are held by such men as Heffelfinger, McClung, Hinkey, Butterworth, Thorn, Chamberlain, Brown, McBride and Glass.

Yale has long relied on the tackle-back play to gain the ground for the team on offense. The tackle is called back and his place is taken by one of the half backs, as a rule. Straight football of the regular character has always formed the basic principle of the Yale attack.

On defense, Yale preserves strictly regular formation. The ends play out wide, the tackles are also at considerable distance out and the three backs are used to support the line.

Yale teams have always maintained positions of prominence in the football world, and Yale graduates have inculcated the football principles in vogue at New Haven in other colleges all over the country.

WISCONSIN

One of the first of the great western universities to successfully develop football was the University of Wisconsin. Games have been played with all the leading western teams during the history of football at Wisconsin, Michigan, Minnesota and Chicago being the most prominent rivals which the "Badgers" have known.

Among the stars of Wisconsin's many good teams were Larson, Driver, Curtis, Cochems, Lerum, Fogg, Abbott and Bush.

Wisconsin early appreciated the necessity for adequate coaching and, in the comparatively early days of the game in the west, invited Phil King, one of Princeton's most famous players, to journey west to take up the work of developing her team. Mr. King's acceptance was followed by many football successes.

As was logically expected, the Princeton system of play was introduced at Wisconsin by King and has ever since been the general style both on offense and defense, King's work being kept up by his own pupils who returned as coaches in later years.

On offense the ends play well out and the backs are relied on to bear the large share of the attack. On defense a strictly regular formation is employed.

"Michigan on the Offense, Wisconsin on the D..."

PENNSYLVANIA

The University of Pennsylvania has long been one of the foremost schools of the football world and, in the early days of the game, has, with Harvard, Yale and Princeton, been one of the "Big Four" institutions in its position of prominence. Football relations have been maintained with Harvard practically since 1881 ; with Yale from 1879 to 1894, and with Princeton from 1876 to 1894. The game has been played at Pennsylvania every year since it became known in any systematized form in the United States. For years the season has closed at Pennsylvania with the annual Thanksgiving Day game with Cornell.

Among the players who have made the elevens of Pennsylvania famous are such men as Gelbert, Knipe, Osgood, Brooke, Woodruff, Hare, Minds, Overfield and McCracken.

Woodruff, who for many years coached the Pennsylvania teams, brought out the famous guards-back play as a method of attack, and for this play and its variations Pennsylvania's teams were long famous. Later it has developed into the tackle-back play, which is a refinement of the Woodruff idea.

On offense and defense alike is the Pennsylvania play distinctively original, for, when the opponents have the ball, the Penn eleven plays in compact order, the ends drawn in and the tackles close to the guards. The ends of Penn are invariably sent into a play with the idea of breaking it up before it has well started, reliance being placed on the backs and tackles to get the runners. The tackles themselves play close and charge forward and toward the center on defensive.

CHICAGO

The elevens from the University of Chicago have always been prominent contenders for honors on the western gridirons. While Chicago's universal rival has always been Michigan, and these schools have maintained football relations ever since the founding of Chicago, the teams from the latter instituion have always taken part in the sectional rivalry which exists with Illinois and Northwestern, besides keeping up an intermittent alliance with Wisconsin and the University of Minnesota.

Chicago alumni recount with pride the deeds of such football heroes as Herschberger, Kennedy, Hammill, Slaker, Sheldon, Henry and Speik.

Coached throughout Chicago's entire athletic history by Alonzo A. Stagg, her elevens have developed a versatility on attack which has always been remarkable. The famous "whoa back" play is a portion of the offense and a general shifting formation in the various plays is always in evidence.

No particular form of defense characterizes Chicago, judged from a basis of the method of play of its various elevens, but the defense generally includes a combination of three men back of the line, shifting to two as the style of attack of the opponents shows to be necessary.

Chicago's teams have also been famous almost every year for the possession of some member with remarkable ability at punting and securing goals from the field.

MICHIGAN ON THE OFFENSE, CHICAGO ON THE DEFENSE.

THE ARMY AND NAVY

For many years the annual games between the elevens representing the United States government's military and naval schools have created great interest in football circles. Both at West Point and Annapolis teams have been maintained since the early history of the game and the annual contest, which is played on the Saturday following Thanksgiving, is always one of the athletic events of the year.

In spite of the relatively small number of men in attendance at each of the government schools, the high class of their students permits of the gathering of a very formidable eleven in each institution and the games annually compare very favorably in skill with any played by the larger university teams. Both teams regularly play preliminary contests with many of the larger schools and the West Point schedule has long been considered the most formidable of any eleven in the country.

Generally speaking, West Point plays the Yale style of game and Annapolis the Princeton system. Most of the coaches of the respective teams have been drawn from these two institutions, Yale men having had charge almost invariably at West Point, while such Princeton stars of former years as Cochran and Edwards have had charge of the Annapolis teams.

STANFORD AND CALIFORNIA

What Yale and Princeton are to the Atlantic states,
Stanford and California are to the Pacific slope. The
sectional isolation of these two large universities has bound
them close together in athletic ties and the annual game
between the two elevens representing these institutions is
the athletic event of the year west of the Rockies.

Stanford has been coached largely by graduates of the
Yale school of play, while California has received her instruction in football very largely from Princeton men.
Very naturally, such coaches as Walter Camp, "Pop" Bliss,
Harry Cross, Chamberlain and others have developed a
distinctively Yale style at Stanford, while "King" Kelly
and Cochran of Princeton have promulgated the Nassau
doctrine on the gridiron of California. Yost and Brooke
have also coached at Stanford, while such well known stars
in their day as Heffelfinger, Gill, Butterworth and Brown
have coached California teams.

Athletic relations on the gridiron have been maintained
between Stanford and California ever since 1891, and games
have also been played between the Pacific coast teams and
elevens from institutions farther east who have made a
post-season tour to the Pacific slope. In all of these games
the Californians from both institutions have shown their
ability to play the game well.

STANFORD ON THE OFFENSE, CALIFORNIA UNIVERSITY ON THE DEFENSE—SAN FRANCISCO, CALIFORNIA.

Football in the south, like football in the west, was taken direct from the game as it originated in the eastern colleges. As early as 1888 a number of schools in the south had football teams, and there has been a general increase of interest in the game until now it is universally recognized in colleges, high schools and preparatory schools south of the Mason and Dixon line. Public interest has been excited in the game until now the south, in all her festivity, gathers around the gridiron to witness the contest between two well known colleges. And as the colleges grow older and as their crowds grow more numerous the time will come when football games will draw as large attendance as is being drawn in similar cities in the north and east.

After the entrance of the game into the southern colleges, the schools depended, like the schools of the west, upon eastern men for coaches. At present a great many of the schools have engaged coaches who have played during their course upon the teams of the well known western institutions. The game as it is now played in the east has markedly different characteristics from the game as it is played in the west. There is more so-called open play in the west, less of compact formations and of the slow pull-together game. Another characteristic of the western game, as distinguished from the eastern, consists of faster consecutive execution of the plays. Therefore much interest is evidenced in the south when teams representing the eastern and western systems meet in contest.

It was thought by many that football would not be popular in the south, the warmth of the climate being assigned as the cause. This has not proved to be true.

Vanderbilt University Football Team Lined Up on the Offense—Right Tackle B...

Position to hold ball for around end throw. Fingers well over the end, arm straight. Bring right foot forward, turning body at the same time throw is made.

PREPARING THE MATERIAL

PASSING, STARTING, CATCHING, KICKING, ETC.

It is useless to attempt the construction of a successful football machine until the raw material in the form of the individual players has been thoroughly developed in the fundamentals of the game. The work on each player must include a thorough course in the rudiments of the game. Each man must be quick and accurate in passing and catching; like a sprinter in starting; sure in kicking and tackling; certain in his ability to carry the ball; capable in blocking and making holes; swift in breaking through; adequate in the knowledge of how to use the straight arm and how to avoid it; certain in interference and quick to fall on the ball.

When the individuals have mastered these details and not until then can the material be collected and the whole machine be assembled for successful work. The illustrations and advice which will follow are given to aid in the development of the players along these rudimentary lines.

PASSING

Passing the ball properly from one player to another is very essential for a successful offense. The ball cannot be handled by the receiver of the pass unless it comes to him at the right time and in the proper form. More of the fumbling in a game is due to poor passing than to any error of the one receiving the ball. There are several forms of passing in practical use; the underhand pass, the underhand spiral, the full-arm throw or pass around the end,

Position to hold the ball just before making under-hand pass—
Arm should swing forward like a pendulum, fingers well around
the end to make it revolve properly when passed.

the spiral throw or pass, the pass from the quarter back in the nature of a toss to a half back on a run around the end and the handing of the ball to a player for a line plunge. There are six illustrations used in connection with this article to show the proper form necessary to execute these passes properly and accurately.

Passing is like any other department of the game in that it requires constant and painstaking practice for one to become proficient. In making the pass the player must be sure that it is not too hard nor too slow. Especially is this true when the pass is a short one. One of the main causes of fumbling by the recipient of the ball is the fact that the pass did not come at the proper height. It is very hard to handle a pass that comes about knee high or at the point of the shoulder. The proper place to receive a pass and the point where it can be easily handled is at the waist. Every man who is a candidate for a football team should master all the forms of passing and receiving the ball. By this work he will become familiar with the ball and will learn to handle it with ease and accuracy.

UNDER-HAND PASS

For the under-hand pass, place the ball in the hand as above, fingers well over the end; swing the arm forward and, as the ball leaves the hand, cause it to turn end over end rapidly, as it can be controlled much better. As in every pass, learn to make the ball go just where you wish it. Never pass indifferently.

ROUND-ARM THROW

In passing the ball by a round-arm throw, take the end of the ball in the palm of the hand, ball extended up and down the arm as shown in the illustration; bring the arm around horizontally and, at the same time, turning the body

The upper position shows how to hold ball for spiral throw. Lower position for spiral pass.

around on the left foot as the ball leaves the hand, cause it to revolve rapidly on its shorter axis. In making this pass, select the place to which the ball should go and make it go where you wish. Control is an essential in all passing.

SPIRAL PASS

For the spiral pass, take the ball in the hand as shown above and swing the arm forward as the pendulum of a clock. As the swing is about finished, pull the hand around and over the ball, causing it to revolve on its axis on the same plan as does a spiral kick. This pass, with practice, can be made quickly and accurately. Its value lies in the fact that it can be passed through, with and against the wind and is very easily handled by the receiver.

SPIRAL THROW

In executing the spiral throw, place the ball on the hand as in the illustration. The ball should lie diagonally across the palm from the base of the thumb to the end of the little finger. The arm should be brought around forward in a horizontal line and, just as the ball leaves the hand, it should be caused to revolve on its axis by suddenly jerking the hand around under the ball and to the left. The oval will thus be made to rotate like a spiral kick. The end of the ball that is shown ahead in the picture must be kept ahead all the time. The ball in this manner can be thrown with ease from 30 to 40 yards. The revolution of the ball on its axis should be rapid.

This pass can be made with, against or across the wind and, with practice, the player can control its distance and direction almost as well as if the oval were a baseball.

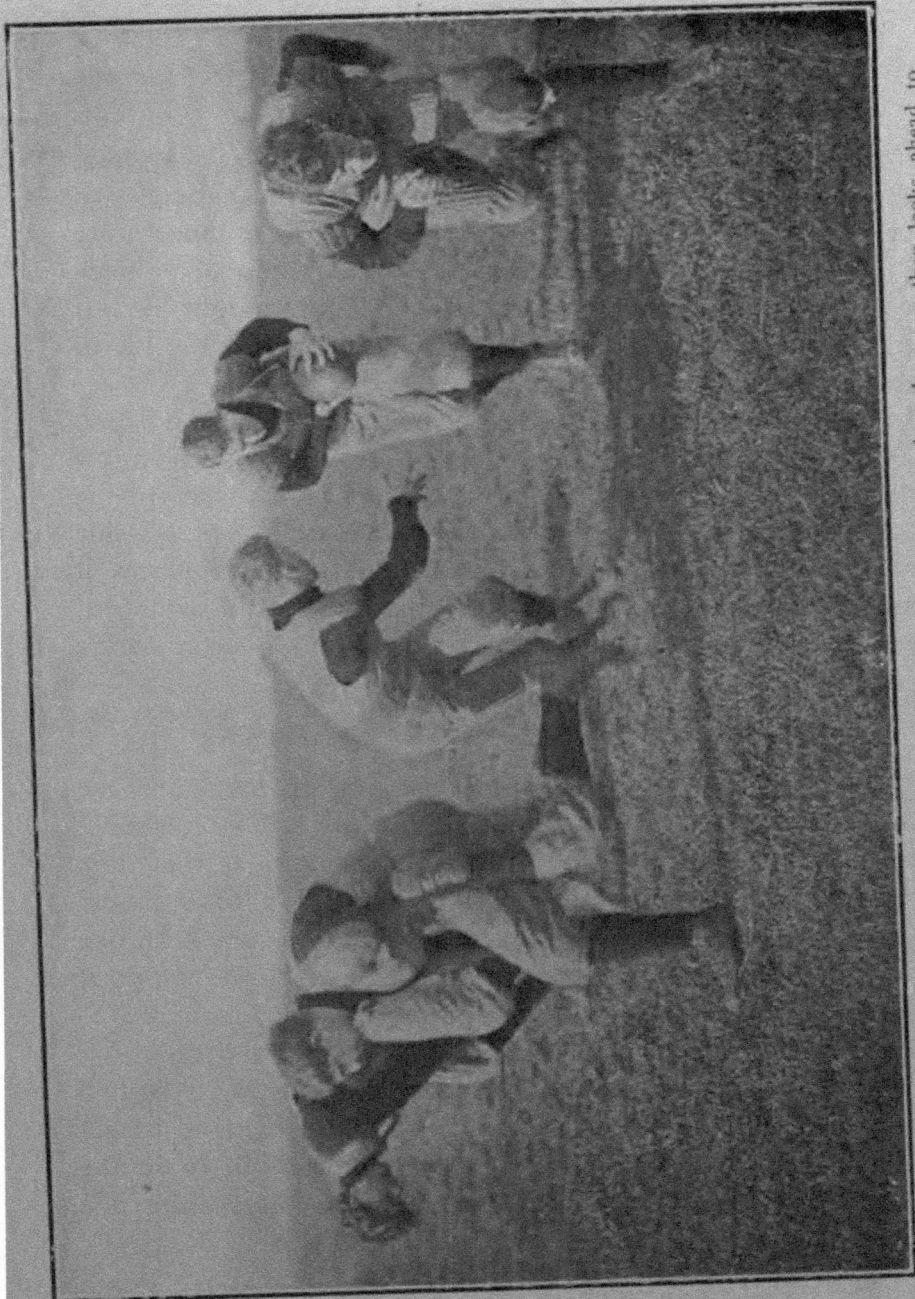

Passing to half back for run around end—Quarter watches back as he makes the pass, then looks ahead to form interference.

PASSING TO PLAYER FOR LINE PLUNGE

The quarter back in passing to the full back for a line plunge through the center should, if the full back is going through on the right side, bring his right foot back almost behind his left. This will give the full back an opportunity to go straight at the point of attack and the quarter back will not be in his way, as he would be if he brought his left foot around. The ball should be placed low, in the pit of the stomach with the right hand.

No player can buck the line as he should if the ball is given to him high. It must come to him low and be carried low after he receives it. The full back should not reach for the ball with his hands but should carry them almost by his side and grasp the ball instantly as the quarter back places it against his body. If he reaches his hands and arms out for the ball he will often interfere with the quarter back's placing the ball properly.

PASS TO BACK FOR STRAIGHT BUCK

The quarter back in making the pass to the half back for a straight plunge into the line, on his left side, should turn around and take a full step to the left, at the same time making the pass to the half back. The pass should be made in the nature of a toss. This can be done with one or two hands, whichever way the quarter finds he can do it the better. The toss must be made quickly to avoid a forward pass. The ball should be passed low, a little lower than the waist. No player can buck the line low if the ball comes to him high. The runner must straighten up to get a high pass and before he can get down he will be in the line. The quarter should look at the runner in making the pass.

Pass to half back for straight plunge through line—Quarter passing it low—Half not reaching hands or arms out so as to interfere with the pass.

PASS TO HALF BACK FOR AROUND THE END

On the work of a quarter back in his passing to the other players for a run outside of tackle or around the end depends largely the success of the play. No player can get away rapidly when the passing is erratic. The ball should always be passed at the outside hip and just ahead of the runner. If the pass is at the inside hip it will slow the runner up when, instead, the main purpose should be to keep him coming hard all the time. The pass should be made by a quick toss. The quarter should get the ball to the runner instantly and then get into the interference himself. As the pass is made he should look at the player who is to receive it. The ball should not be passed underhanded but quickly and with a round-arm motion.

CATCHING

Good catchers are scarce in the game of football. This is because they do not devote the time and attention necessary to become proficient. The oblong shape of the ball and the fact that it is inflated with air makes its flight uncertain to some extent, yet with practice a player can learn to judge just where the ball will fall and to be there in the proper place to receive it. Until the members of a team become reliable and steady in handling punts and passes the eleven will be uncertain in all its play. Football is a game that is full of passes and punts and each time the ball is passed or punted it must be handled accurately or the play will fail.

In catching punts or long passes the direction of the wind must be taken into consideration. If the ball is coming with the wind it is sure to go farther than it promised in the first of its flight. The height of the kick and the force of

POSITION ONE.—Form for catching a punt. Hands should be in this position as ball approaches; right hand must be under ball.

the wind will determine how much to allow for this additional distance. Then again, the kind of kick, spiral or floater, will have much to do with its distance and direction. When catching a spiral, if the front end of the ball is watched closely, its direction and distance can be easily judged. The player wishing to make the catch should be back of the place where the ball will alight on the ground. He should never be too far under the ball as it comes down, for if it gets over the head of the catcher it will probably roll a great distance. If the player is just back of where the ball will fall he can easily move forward at the last moment, make the catch on the run and be going toward the opponents' goal.

FORM FOR MAKING THE CATCH

Position 1.

Position 1 shows the proper form of the hands and arms as they are first extended to receive the ball on a punt or pass. The lower or right hand is to form the bottom of the pocket into which the ball is to fall.

Position 2.

The ball should be so judged that it will fall into a pocket, formed by the two hands and the body. The right hand will form the bottom, the left hand the outside, and the body the inside. The arms are not used in making the catch. The hands and body do the work. The ball must be watched closely. The hands should come in toward the body from Position 1. This will help bring the ball to the right place.

Position 3.

This illustrates exactly how the ball should be caught. This same form can be used to catch the ball at either side of the body, merely by shifting the hands. It can be used

to catch the ball when it is high or low. The one hand
must always be under the ball to keep it from passing

Position Two.—Form for catching. The ball should fall into the pock
formed by the hands and body; right hand forming the bottom of pock
left hand the outside, and body the inside.

through, while the other hand must be used to prevent the ball from rebounding as it strikes the body.

The player bent on making the catch must so meet the ball that it will come into the hands properly and against the body at the right height. The ball will often change its course quickly and it will be necessary for the catcher to shift just as readily to meet it.

A careful study of the illustrations will show the proper form to use in catching the ball. This form will be found sufficient to handle all kinds of kicks and high passes. The same principle can be used in receiving passes that come straight toward the catcher, with the exception that the hands are held lower and directly ahead, instead of upward.

POSITION IN STARTING

The two illustrations which accompany this chapter show better than any detailed description the position to be assumed for starting by the regular backfield men or the members of the line who may be called into the backfield on any formations. In attaining the proper form the football player should guard against the two common faults in this respect. Either the hips are held too high or the body is not thrown far enough forward, with not enough weight on the hands. In the former case there is a lack of driving power to the start which is often fatal. In the latter the speed of the start is impaired for the player, for when his body is not well forward he loses the benefit of this marked aid to the momentum which he should attain in the first two or three strides.

No general rule can be laid down for the exact pose in starting. This is occasioned by the differences in the build of the men who are playing the game. The player can find out by actual experience the plan which best suits his phy-

POSITION THREE—Just as the hands, body and ball should be when ball is caught.

sical makeup, guarding against placing his feet too far apart laterally, or one foot too far ahead of the other. Generally speaking, the position of a sprinter on his mark is the proper form for the player to assume, except that the feet should be wider apart and the rear foot brought up farther forward. The weight of the body should be principally on the hands, so that the instant the hands are removed from the ground the weight of the body will assist him in getting under rapid motion. All this requires an immense amount of practice before perfection can be attained. Only by continual and conscientious effort can speed be attained in this respect.

The linemen, generally speaking, will find that their position for starting will be a modified form of that in use by the backs. The proximity of their positions to their opponents requires that the men in the line take a position considerably modified from that of the occupants of the backfield. Here, in addition to the necessity for a quick advance straight ahead or to either side, the player must guard against a sudden jerk forward from his immediate opponent. The weight of his body must therefore be less on his hands and more on his feet in order to guard against being over-balanced. The proper position for starting in the line is thoroughly indicated in the illustrations used to show the different offensive formations and the positions assumed for starting at the charging machine.

Proper form in starting is half the battle when the time comes for actual play, as no player can expect to handle an opponent of equal skill unless he is well up in the art. Further, if the occupants of the backfield are not taught to get under way rapidly and together a large share of the momentum on offense is sacrificed by the failure. The acquisition of a quick, strong start is well worth the trouble that is necessary to attain it.

Showing two forms used by backs in starting. Some can get away better by one and some by the other. Practice both and adapt the one best suited.

KICKING

Kicking is one of the most interesting features of football. To attain success in this department of the game requires considerable skill. One cannot become proficient as a kicker without constant and careful practice. The oval shape of the ball requires that it be dropped to the foot at the proper angle and time.

The value of a good and reliable kicker to a team cannot be estimated. The difference between two good teams, which gives one the victory over the other, is often the difference in the abilities of its kickers.

Three kinds of kicks are used in football: The punt, drop and place kicks. Six illustrations accompany this chapter; three of them show the proper form to use in punting. Of these, one shows how to hold the ball so that it may be dropped to the foot in the proper manner. Another demonstrates just how the ball should reach the foot, at what distance from the ground and just how far it should be out in front of the body. The other one shows how the kick should be finished.

Two of the other pictures show the form for proficiency in place kicking, one giving the proper position just before the kick, and the other just after the kick is started. The last illustration shows the best and easiest manner of holding the ball before dropping it to the ground for a drop kick.

PUNT

A punt is made by letting the ball drop from the hands and kicking it just before it touches the ground. There are two kinds of punts now in use,—one, the spiral, which all try to acquire, and the other the end-over-end kick, which is very valuable when used with the wind. It is al-

FIGURE ONE.—Form for holding ball just before it is dropped to the foot.

most useless when used against the wind, however, as it cannot be driven into the face of a breeze nearly so far as the spiral.

The first faculty to be acquired in order to become a good and reliable punter is the proper form. This is often overlooked in order to get distance at once. With form once mastered, speed and distance will be sure to follow.

SPIRAL

The following is the form for a spiral: Standing in the position illustrated in Figure 1 on punting, step forward and to the right with the right foot for about two feet and follow this with the left foot which is carried about one yard and slightly to the right. Then drop the ball to the right foot as it is swung forward, toe turned down as in Figure 2, and finish the kick as in Figure 3. The leg should be rigid as the foot strikes the ball. The knee joint should be locked and straight. The ball should come to the foot in almost exactly the same position in which it is held in the hands in Figure 1, and should be laid out on the instep as it is kicked. Do not throw it. The ball must come to the foot in this way and at the right time, or the punt will be inaccurate. There must be no "fluke kicks" in the games.

Another reason why the ball should be practically laid out on the foot is the fact that, when kicking on a wet or windy day, there is not much chance for the ball to change its position between the time it leaves the hand and reaches the foot. In kicking, the ball must be watched all the time, for no one can hit the object at which he aims unless he has his eye on it. The ball must not be kicked from a point too near the kicker, for that will yield a result very much in the nature of a throw. It should be a little above knee-high to the kicker at the moment when it meets the foot.

FIGURE TWO.—How the foot should meet the ball, distance ball should be out in front of body and height ball should be from ground. Ball should hit the instep.

It must be struck by the foot near the center and the foot driven straight ahead for an instant with a quick finish toward the point of the left shoulder. This will give the ball the rotary motion of the spiral.

Practice this form for some time, gradually putting more and more speed and force into the kick.

The direction of the kick, as well as the height of the ball, should always be kept in mind. It is not the force that is put into the whole motion of the kick that will give it distance, but the snap that is put into the leg at the moment it strikes the ball. The steps taken just before the ball is kicked must not carry the kicker much forward toward the center. If this is the case the kicker will be up against his own line and in a position where the kick can be easily blocked by the opponents.

The steps should be short. There is no necessity for running a foot race before the ball is kicked. It is the force and energy put into the kicking leg at the moment of contact that will give distance to the kick, not the two steps before the final swing of the leg.

The same general directions may be followed when learning the end-over-end punt, with the exception of the manner in which the ball is dropped to the foot.

PLACE KICK

The place kick is made by placing the ball in position on the ground and kicking it from this location. The value of a good place kicker to the team cannot be estimated for, by his work, the game may be won or lost. Place kicking has almost entirely taken the place of drop kicking, because it is more accurate. It is used to convert touchdowns into goals, to kick goals from the field, to kick off, and is often used to kick out after a touchback, instead of punting.

There are two illustrations used in connection with this article to show the form and style necessary in order to become a proficient and accurate place kicker. The skillful execution of a place·kick depends almost as much upon the

FIGURE THREE.—The position of leg, foot and body just after ball has left the foot. The kick should be followed out.

holder of the ball as upon the kicker himself. Great care should be used by the former in placing the ball upon the ground in the exact position desired by the kicker. The holder of the ball must not change its position in the least in removing his hands or fingers from under it. He must not remove his top hand but must permit the kicker to kick the ball while the upper hand is yet in place. The holder of the ball must be steady and cool.

In making the place kick, the kicker's position should be about four feet behind the ball. He should draw an imaginary line directly through the center of the goal bar, through the center of the ball, and the kicking leg should be in a direct line with the center of the ball and the center of the goal bar. In other words, a straight line, drawn from the right or kicking toe through the center of the ball, should pass directly across the center of the goal bar.

The kicker's position on short kicks should be not over four feet behind the ball. If he stands too far away it is harder for him to approach and kick exactly as he should, and he acquires no advantage by being so far back. After the kicker has assumed his proper position and the ball is ready, he should step forward about six inches with his right foot and then step forward with the left foot until the toe is practically on line with the rear of the ball, but a little to the left. The right toe should then come forward, toe turned down, the kicker's eye in the meanwhile glued to the spot on the ball which he wishes the toe to hit. The right foot should be brought forward along the original line. The kick is made more by the swing of the knee than of the hip. Follow the kick through after the ball has been struck as in Position 2. The feet should travel along the line which the ball is to take. Do not finish as in a punt, but follow the kick through.

When distance is wished, as in an attempt for a goal from the field at the 40-yard line, the distance of the kicker behind the ball should be increased and more of the swing of the leg from the hip should be put into the kick, to add force and distance. The same observations in the "line of kick" should be followed when a kick is to be made from any position on the field, whether from near the center or near the sidelines. The holder of the ball and the kicker should work together enough to become thoroughly in touch with each other. Some kickers require that the ball should be almost vertical in its position on the ground;

Position to assume just before ball is touched to the ground. Care must be taken to place ball on ground in same position as held. Kicker stands close for short kick.

others that the top be tilted back toward the kicker. What is best suited to the individual kicker can be learned only by constant practice.

In kicking goals from touchdowns there is no necessity

As the ball is kicked from the ground the kicker should have his
   toe turned down and the eyes on the spot he wishes his toe
   to hit. Follow kick through toward center of goal bar.

for hurry. Take plenty of time, observing carefully the
condition of wind and weather. There is much difference
in kicking a dry, new ball, and a wet, heavy one, that has
been used perhaps throughout the greater part of a game.
More care is necessary when the kick is against the wind,
than when with it.

Summed up, the important points in a place kick are
to see that the ball is placed correctly on the ground; that

the kicker observe the ball closely in making his kick, instead of directing his attention to the goal bar; that he kicks the ball with the toe turned down, and that the kick is made on the straight line to the center of the goal bar.

DROP KICK

A drop kick is made by letting the ball fall from the hands and kicking it the instant it strikes the ground. Although this kick is not in very common use, a team may possess someone who can become very accurate in kicking goals from the field by this method. Any team which includes a good and accurate drop kicker has an advantage over one using a place kicker, in that there is one more man who can be used to protect the kick.

The form of holding a ball is shown in an accompanying illustration. It is immaterial how the ball is held in the hand but it is very important that it should come to the ground in the proper position. This position is one that varies with the different kickers but the one suited to most players allows the ball to strike the ground in an almost vertical position with the top slanting toward the kicker. As in place kicking, the ball must be kicked by the toe and closely watched as the kick is made. The direction of the goal should be fully known before the player receives the ball. The ball must be hit the instant it reaches the ground. Do not wait until the ball has rebounded and catch it on the instep. No one can be accurate who kicks with the instep.

To become proficient as a drop kicker will require long, faithful practice. Care should be taken in learning the art to acquire height and direction, as practically all the drop kicking must be done from behind a scrimmage line and, unless the ball rises instantly, there is much danger of the kick being blocked or at least interfered with.

The ball just before it is dropped to the ground for a drop kick. The foot and ball must meet the instant the ball touches the ground. Watch the ball in drop kicking.

TACKLING

Proper form in tackling is a necessity to the football player. The player on the opposing eleven who is carrying the ball must be firmly grasped and thrown to the ground or he will keep up his progress toward your goal. Tackling, generally, can be separated into two divisions—long tackling and short tackling. In each case, however, the aim of the tackler should be directed at a point midway between the hips and the knees. He should get both arms securely round the legs of the runner and should grasp firmly and with a determination not to be shaken off.

The long tackle is employed in the open field, when the runner has an opportunity to dodge to either side. In such a case the tackler should aim first of all to get in the direct path of the man with the ball. When within diving distance the tackler should launch himself into the air as a swimmer leaps into the water, giving every possible speed of spring to his effort and wrapping his arms round the runner's legs below the hips. He should guard against diving too low, for this may enable the runner to elude him, either by hurdling or wriggling out of his grasp. The tackle should always be low enough, however, to pin the legs of the runner together, thereby bringing him to earth. The resistance of the runner as he falls will protect the tackler from any possible injury from striking the ground, as the runner will act as a buffer.

If the tackler finds it impossible to get in the path of the runner he should get within reaching distance from the side and then make his dive from a distance of about his own length. In this case the tackler should always aim to get his head in front of the runner, thus making the tackle more secure through the added impediment that is offered to the progress of the man with the ball.

The short tackle is largely confined to the tackling of runners in the line. In such case, the runner is usually within reaching distance and the tackler under less rapid motion. As the two come together the tackler should go into his man low, grasping him between the hips and knees and launching himself forward and upward toward the opponents' goal at the very moment of the tackle, the purpose being the securing of an added impetus which will carry the runner back. If it is possible, the tackler should launch his weight from a position which will allow him to strike the runner in a position which will lift him off his feet. This will make the tackle all the more effective.

An effective tackle, shown in one of the illustrations which accompany this chapter, is one made from behind. This is frequently possible when a forward has broken through the line just behind the path of the play. It is also employed in the open field when a runner has passed the first line of defense and is going down the field.

CARRYING THE BALL

The art of taking a secure hold of the ball when called upon for a gain and retaining its possession from the time it is received from the center or quarter back till the play is ended is an important feature of football, but one often overlooked. How many times, by one disastrous fumble, is a team that has apparently won been forced to see its colors trailed in defeat! How many backs, fast, strong and brilliant have been tried again and again only to be discarded because of this one fault!

Regardless of its ground-gaining ability, little is gained by any team unless its members know how to keep a firm grasp of the ball throughout the progress of a play, for one fumble is usually enough to hand over the coveted pigskin

The flying tackle from behind. A touchdown may often be...

to the opponents and with it an opportunity to punt it back again for many yards, necessitating a second fight over ground previously battled for and won.

There are three correct methods of carrying the ball, all of which are accurately shown in the accompanying illustrations. Two of these are for use when the play is designed to pierce the opponents' line, while the other is for running in the open field or circling the end.

In all plunges into the line the ball should be held tightly against the pit of the runner's stomach, both hands and arms being used. There are two positions in which the ball can be held, some runners preferring to carry it straight across the body, while others find the vertical position more secure. Regarding a choice, each player should suit himself. He should always bear in mind, however, at all stages of the play, the absolute necessity for maintaining the firm grasp by both hands and arms on the ball. Often, after a plunge into the line, a runner, when being thrown, will throw out one arm to save himself and thus he often loses his hold on the ball or allows an opponent to steal it. The player should school himself never to forget his duty to this extent, for it not only places the ball in serious jeopardy but increases, rather than diminishes, his liability to injury, as the arm, thrown loose from the body, is very liable to fracture in the mass of men that is piling up on him as he is tackled.

For a run round the end or for one in the open field, the runner should grasp the ball with the "outside" arm, leaving the other to assist him in stiff-arming tacklers. The ball, as the illustration shows, should be held tightly against the body, the rear end securely pressed against the body and well under the upper arm, while the forward end is grasped by the fingers and wrist. The fingers should be well over the

Two forms for holding ball on plunges through the line—Both are good; ada
one best suited to the individual.

end and should assist in pulling the ball back into the pocket formed by the body and elbow. If the ball is held in this way, with plenty of strength exerted all the time to keep it rigidly in position, fumbles or loss of the ball by any attempted "theft" will be entirely obviated. It is always best, however, for the runner to make doubly sure against a fumble when tackled, by clasping the top of the ball with the free hand, as he is thrown to the ground. This also prevents possible injury to the free arm, bringing it up under the runner where it will be protected by his body.

Frequently a combination of the line-plunging and open-field holds of the ball is desirable, this being especially effective on such occasions as when an attempt at the line has proven so successful that the runner is entirely clear of the first line of defense. In this case he will be wise to shift his hold of the ball to that employed in a run round the end, thus bringing his free arm to a position where it can be used in the run through the open field which is to follow.

The secure grasp on the ball which must be the acquirement of every successful ground gainer should not be a matter of thought. He should learn to take it intuitively the moment the oval is passed to him, and this requires practice and patience. It is only by repeated trials in actual play and by faithful application to his work that the player can reach this stage of efficiency; but the art once learned will not be forgotten and is well worth the pains needed to acquire it.

Proper position to hold ball on runs around end or in open field—
Rear end of ball should be well under upper arm and the fingers should have a firm hold on forward end of ball; elbow
should hold ball close against body.

BLOCKING AND MAKING HOLES

The first duty of the forwards of a football eleven is to learn thoroughly and be able to put into practice sure methods of blocking their opponents, in order that the latter may not be able to break through the line and tackle runners before plays can be fairly set in motion. The object of football is to score points and no team is able to do this unless the backs receive the protection they have a right to expect from the men who are playing in the line.

There are two methods of blocking an opponent, although these two permit of numerous variations. Opponents can be blocked with the shoulder or with the hip. Blocking with the arms is attempted at times, but this comes dangerously close to holding and is, as well, less effective for the purpose desired.

Generally speaking, the blocker should keep as close as possible to the man whom he is to keep out of the play. He is thus all the better enabled to watch his every move and be ready to anticipate it. He should study the position of his opponent in each play and follow him in his every move. While the opponent has the advantage in one sense, being able to use his arms in getting through, the blocker has one marked superiority over him, in that he has secured, through the signals of his quarter back, an accurate knowledge of the play that is to come and the direction in which it is to travel. Accordingly, he knows best which side to guard and the length of time which he will have to detain his opponent. Usually this is but a fraction of a second. The blocker should, the moment the ball is snapped, jump into his opponent, striking him squarely with the shoulder, if possible. He must keep his feet well under him to avoid a possible sudden jerk which would throw him forward on his face. In case the shoulder compact should be avoided

Upper—Blocking with hip. Lower—Blocking with shoulder.

by the opponent in any way, the blocker should endeavor to stop his man by interposing his hips. Often a player can wrap himself about an opponent by this method, so that the motions of the latter are completely checked for a moment, which will be time enough for the play to have gotten well under way.

MAKING HOLES

Closely allied to, and in fact almost identical with blocking, is the making of holes in the line, through which to allow the backs to travel toward the opponents' goal. In this, as in blocking, the main purpose rests in so charging the opponent that he is momentarily put out of the play. The added necessity here is, however, that he shall be put out of the play in a certain direction, thus requiring more finesse and more certain strength and rapidity, in order not only to prevent the opponent from tackling the runner, but also to get him out of the way of the man with the ball, who is coming to a certain point.

The forward who is on the offensive, keeping as close as possible and making use of every inch of room allowed him, should, as before, act instantly and with all the strength at his command. He knows where the play is coming and should maneuver to get all the advantage of position for use in the crucial moment. He should watch his opponent's eyes and, the moment the ball is snapped, should charge forward, rising the moment he meets the enemy and endeavoring to get his own shoulder against the opponent's breast, if such be possible. The impact should carry the opponent back and to the side, the idea being the opening of a lane through which may come the runner with the ball. Aim to get under the opponent always, if this be possible. If he plays very low, aim to get him in such a way that he

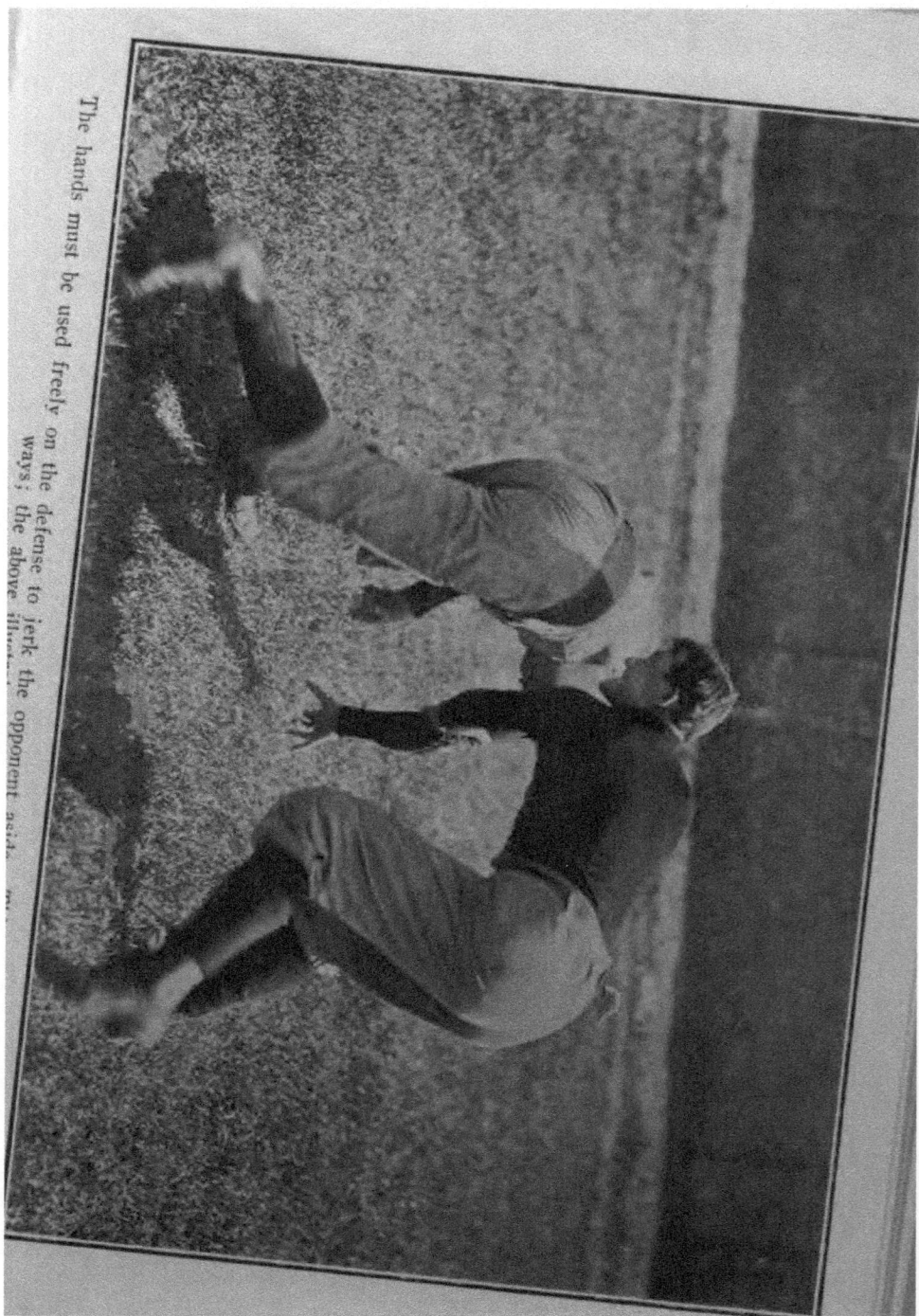

The hands must be used freely on the defense to jerk the opponent aside,
ways; the above illustra... Th...

may first be turned aside and then forced back.

Constant study of an opponent will assist in determining the methods by which he may most effectively be put out of a play. If he is found to be more vulnerable on one side than on the other, the quarter back who is directing the play of the team of which you are a member will become cognizant of the fact and will send the plays at the point where the hole is easiest to obtain.

BREAKING THROUGH

The most effective method of breaking up the play of an opposing team is illustrated when a team possesses forwards who are able to penetrate the opposing line, starting the moment the ball is snapped and either tackling the man with the ball or so throwing his interference into such confusion that the runner is tackled the moment he reaches the line of scrimmage or even before. Trouble without measure can be meted out to an opposing team in this manner, when there is a forward or two capable of breaking through, and every play directed by the opponents should be a signal for instant effort to this end on the part of the defensive team.

The ability to break through an opposing line is not one inherent on mere brute force by any means. It requires mental ability in sizing up the opponent in the way, skill in avoiding his attempt to block and, above all, rapidity in thought and motion. A mere "beefy" man will be made to appear a novice at the game by a strong, resourceful player, well versed in the art.

The forward whose line is on the defense should aim to keep his opponent at arm's length until the moment the ball is snapped. The team on the defensive has the use of hands and arms and should employ this advantage to the

The tackle should keep the end away from him, also the tackle. This can be done if the hands are used skillfully.

utmost. The standard method of breaking through the line is to charge forward immediately, the moment the ball is snapped, arms out stiff and body low down. The opponent should be pushed to one side and the runner is very likely to be at the mercy of the man who has gotten through. Another method is to catch the opponent by the outside arm. When this grasp is secured the opponent will jerk back, which will often pull you through. It may also be possible to pull him to one side, which will enable you to pass by. Still another plan is to strike the opponent on one side, immediately shifting the attack to the other. The same purpose is often attained by making a feint at one side and then changing the line of attack. If the opponent is playing very low he may be hurdled, caught by the head and pushed or pulled in either direction.

All methods of breaking through, tried with success in the early stages of the game, may fail as the opponent learns to anticipate them. The forward should then vary his style, always producing some new trick which will constantly keep the enemy guessing.

Get the jump on the other fellow. Don't let your opponent get to your body. Don't go through too high. Don't forget to use hands and arms whenever their use will assist in getting through. Charge forward all the time.

USE OF STIFF ARM AND HOW TO AVOID IT

The proper use of the stiff arm by a runner in the open field is an acquisition which will be found well nigh invaluable to a back who is carrying the ball in a dash down the field. As the runner sees that he is about to be tackled he can suddenly shoot out his free arm, palm open, meeting the charge of the tackler with the arm stiff and rigid, often

Showing the use of the stiff arm to avoid being tackled. The hand can be placed on head, shoulder, or often the body. The tackler can be thrown aside or side-stepped.

turning him aside to such an extent that he either entirely
misses the tackle or is sufficiently foiled in his purpose to
allow the runner to free himself without stopping and to
continue on his way toward the opponents' goal. The
straight arm can be directed toward the opponent's breast,
if the latter is coming high, or toward his head or shoulder,
if he is making his effort in a crouched position. Continual practice will develop a proficiency that will enable
the runner to escape many tackles which, without the stiff
arm, would certainly have brought him to earth.

In delivering the stiff arm the runner should always
aim to conceal his intention as far as possible from the
tackler, avoiding the habit of carrying the arm in an advanced position before the tackler gets close enough to permit its use, and shooting out the arm at exactly the moment
when the opponent attempts the tackle. If the runner's
purpose is divulged in advance, the tackler will be ready
to ward it off and the stiff arm will be of little use.

Use of the stiff arm is confined entirely to runners in
the open field. It is a hindrance, rather than an aid, in line
plunging, where there are possible tacklers on all sides and
the runner's purpose must be, first of all, to force his way
through. When a runner, however, succeeds in getting
through a line into the open field, the stiff arm may enable
him to dispose of a tackler and thereby convert his effort
into a touchdown, as there may then be but one tackler between him and the opponents' goal.

The tackler, in approaching a runner with the ball,
should always bear in mind the possibility of a sudden stiff
arm and should be on his guard against it. He should
meet it with a parry like that which a boxer would employ
against a straight jab from an opponent, brushing the arm
aside and out of his way, generally upward, in his effort

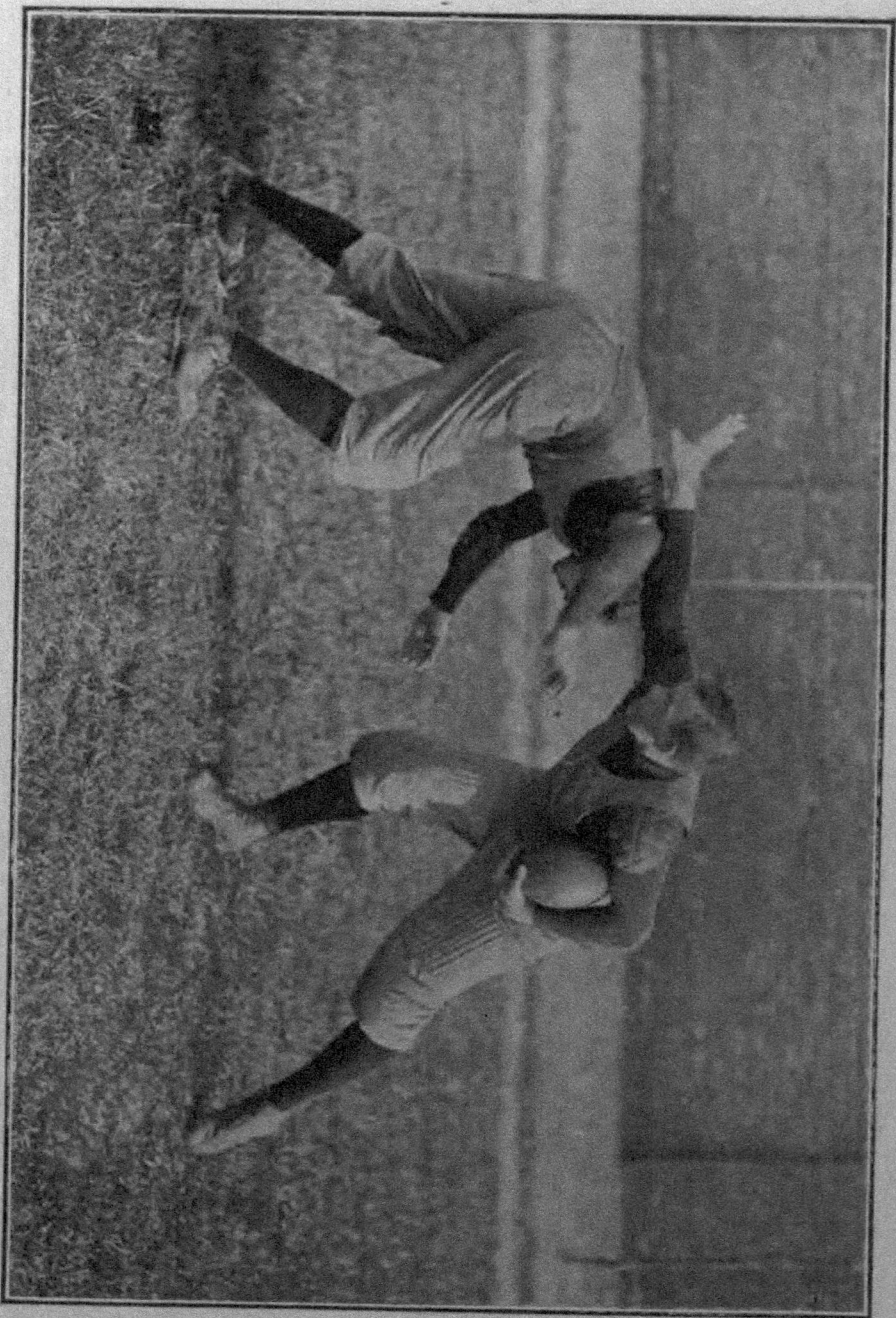

This picture illustrates how the stiff arm can be thrown aside by the tackler using his arm for that purpose, and then going in under it.

to get close to the runner and bring him down. The
tackler should not wait for a hint that the stiff arm is to
be used but should anticipate it on every occasion when it
would be possible for the runner to employ it. He will
thus be enabled to get close to his man and cannot be
brushed to either side, out of the runner's path or to the
ground in front of him, there to be hurdled or side-stepped.

The two illustrations which accompany this chapter
should be of great value in demonstrating the use of the
stiff arm and the way in which a tackler should be able to
avoid it.

WARDING OR INTERFERING

Effective interference, or the warding off of tacklers
from the runner with the ball by the members of his team,
is one of the absolute necessities to success in any offensive
plays not directed as plunges into the opposing line. Any
attempt to carry the ball which in any way develops a contest between the two forces in the open field must be sup-
ported by capable interference or it will signally fail.

The interference whereby possible tacklers are thwarted
in their purpose is accomplished by the knees, body or
shoulders of the interferer, the purpose being to so cast
the person of the interferer between the tackler and the
runner as to put the former out of the play. The portion
of the interferer which can best be used for this end varies
with the attitude in which the contemplative tackler is making his attempt to get at the runner. If the tackler is coming low he can be warded off by the interferer's knees; if
coming in the medium position he can be checked with the
hips; if still higher up, he can be met with the shoulder.

In every case the interferer must aim to meet the tackler
with all his might and must prevent the latter at all events

from forcing him back into the path of the runner with the ball. If he fails in this he is merely an impediment, instead of an assistance to the progress of the ball. When an interferer and a tackler meet, it is one or the other that is going to be put out of the play, and the interferer should see to it that the opponent is brushed aside and the path of the runner cleared of the man whom it is his duty to take care of.

An interferer should always aim to do his work intelligently. He should not wait for the man he is assigned to watch but should anticipate the rush of the opponent. He should never brush by the man but should charge him energetically, to prevent his slipping behind and dragging down the runner. The interferer must see his man and keep him in sight all the time till he is put out of the play.

Out in the open an interferer can frequently save his man from being tackled by a long dive, if it is impossible to reach him in any other way. This form of assistance to the man with the ball is often very effective.

FALLING ON THE BALL

A football player is often called upon to fall on the ball as it lies on the ground or rolls along over the field. If the ball is in motion it may be coming toward the player, going away from him or traveling directly across his front.

If the ball is moving away from the player he should dive for it, lighting on the knees first and falling forward on and around the ball as in Figure 1. The hands and arms should draw the ball securely against the body to prevent any of the opponents obtaining even part possession of it. This they will always try to do. If the ball is bounding so that it can easily be caught off the ground, then the player should catch it. Never pick the ball up if it is lying

Upper picture illustrates how to fall on ball that is coming toward
you. The lower one, when it is going away.

on the ground, however. Always fall on it or someone else will do so. If the ball is rolling along slowly on the ground, the player can still use his hands or arms to gather it in under the body.

When the ball is bounding it must be watched closely, as it will bound irregularly.

If an opponent is about to fall on the ball it is sometimes possible to push him so that he will miss it, and the oval can then be secured for your side. The ball may also at times be successfully kicked out from under an opponent just as he is about to fall on it. If two men are racing for the ball with one of the opponents it is often best for one man to block off the opponent, allowing his own team mate to secure the ball.

In falling on the ball, do not fall with your weight directly on it, as this is likely to produce injury, but break the fall with the knees and elbows. The player must make sure of the ball first and foremost, and must not try to pick it up if there is any chance of losing it to the other side.

The above illustration shows the proper manner to fall on a ball that is fumbled at a player's feet or is rolling towards him. The player should throw his feet directly back and practically "curve up" in front of and around the ball. If the ball is moving, the legs and body together with the hands and arms can be used to pocket it up. The upper part of the body should come to the ground, the left side first if falling as above. If on the other side of the ball, the conditions would be reversed.

The player should practice falling on the ball while it is moving in every conceivable way. Practice should consist of diving and falling on the ball quickly. If the ball is to be secured in a game on a fumble before the opponents, no time can be spent in quietly lying down around it.

INDIVIDUAL POSITIONS

THE END

The position of end calls for notable physical and mental qualities on the part of the player and for a knowledge of the fine points of the game that can result only from long experience. Of all the men on the rush line, his area of play is the widest and his duties the most varied.

There is no rule of weight to which the end must conform, but he must be speedy. An active, resourceful man, with a quick eye, steady nerve and fine judgment, will often surpass a much heavier man in this position, yet for many of the end's duties weight and strength are an advantage, provided that these qualities are coupled with quickness and intelligence.

An end must possess great speed and endurance to enable him to make long dashes up and down the field in pursuit of punts, and occasionally to relieve the back in carrying the ball. He needs strength and weight to enable him to sustain singly, as he frequently must, the charge of several men in a body, and to break up rapidly moving interference. He needs a quick eye, long practice and good judgment to solve the tricks and fake plays of his opponents, for many of these tricks are especially designed for his deception. He must ever be on the alert for plays down the sidelines, that no one may be outside of him to receive a long pass or secure a short kick.

On the offense, when the team lines up, the end takes his place close to his tackle and just opposite the outside hip of the opposing tackle. He must place himself in a good position to aid in boxing up or in blocking out the opposing tackle, and to secure this result there is no better way than to charge hard and low with the shoulder at some point between the hip and knee of the opponent. The end must go into his man hard, else he will be warded off by the hands of the opposing player, who will then slip between him and his tackle.

If the attack is toward his side of the line, the end must aid his tackle in boxing the opposite tackle, in case the point of attack is outside the end position, and in blocking out the opposing tackle when the point of attack is inside the end position. He should pay no attention to the opposing end, leaving that player to be taken care of by the interference coming ahead of the runner. As soon as the runner has safely passed the opponents' line, the end should follow the man with the ball and make himself useful as the occasion permits.

When the attack is made on the opposite side, the end should follow back of his own line, becoming general "safety man." It is his duty to get in promptly to save the ball in case of a fumble, to protect the runner from a rear attack and to pull or shove the runner along or interfere for him, as the opportunity presents itself.

When his team is on the defensive, the work of the end is very different. He takes up a very different position on the line, moving away from his tackle from three to four yards, the distance depending on the formation of the opponents. He should play as closely as possible, just far enough out to make certain he cannot be boxed in. He should not leave much space between himself and the tackle, as this will make a weak point in the defense. Some men play so widely that, figuratively speaking, they need a field glass or a telephone connection to find out what is going on.

The end should get ready for a very quick start, taking

practically the position of a sprinter on his mark, the tips of his fingers just touching the ground, one foot slightly behind the other. The instant the ball is snapped, the end must start, like the sprinter at the crack of the pistol. He should go directly forward from four to six yards, depending on the direction of the opponents' attack, and then turn toward the center of the line. When the play is coming in his direction, the end confronts a situation calling for the exercise of all his physical and mental powers in the highest degree. If the play gets by him, outside, there is a clear field beyond the runner. The end must remember that he is responsible for all the territory outside of his position and he must always turn the runner in toward the center of the line. The end has to meet the charge of several moving men and has to meet it in a way either to break up the interference effectively, thus enabling him to attack the runner, or, failing in this, to compel the runner to turn in towards tackle, where he can be more easily stopped by the other players. It is a situation calling for the greatest intensity of action, as well as for high moral qualities of self-control and courage. The end in this situation must allow no one to block him but must successfully ward off with hands and arms all attacks and, if possible, break through and stop the runner.

When the attack of the opponents is directed at the other side of the line, the end must always follow in behind the opposing line and tackle the runner if possible, watching out, however, for delayed passes and criss-cross plays, especially designed to escape his vigilance and so enable the runner to get around his end. The end must go in quickly and be on hand in case of a fumble by an opponent, but must not be over-anxious and so likely to be fooled when a trick is sprung.

When his own side punts, it is the duty of the end to get down the field with the ball to prevent a return run. In doing this, if the opposing end is blocking on the line of scrimmage, it is better that the end start from his position close to tackle, and go directly down the field, taking care to keep outside of the ball and the man who is catching it. If the opposing end drops back about ten yards, the end should move out a similar distance just before the ball is to be snapped, and should go down from that position, using his hands for warding off the opposing end, who will attempt to block or check him.

In going down on a punt, the end must determine about where the ball will fall by the general movements of the men in the backfield or by snatching a glimpse at the ball over his shoulder as he runs. He should be very careful not to over-run the ball, which he is very likely to do in the case of a short kick. The end should always keep well outside the catcher, so that, if he does not down the man himself, he can at least turn him in toward his own men, who are following down the field close after him.

When the opponents are about to kick, the end should drop back about ten yards and about ten yards outside of a point directly behind his own tackle, prepared to watch out for a fake kick or to go down the field with the opposing end if the kick does take place, interfering with his opponent as he attempts to tackle the catcher. Sometimes it is good policy to block the opposing end just as soon as it can be done, but it is usually more effective to go down the field and interfere with him as he is about to make the tackle, for then he will have no other opportunity to get the runner.

Much more might be said about the duties of the end on offense, but this feature will be fully explained in that portion of the bock devoted to team play.

THE TACKLE

The position of tackle is the most important one on the rush line. The tackle is the "work horse" of the eleven. He is called upon to stop most of the plays of the opponents, since nine-tenths of their attack is aimed at his position or just outside of him. On offense, in the various "tackle-back" or "tackle-over" plays that are so extensively used in the present development of the game, he is required to head the interference or to plunge through the line with the ball like a full back. He has become the important man in every play, and success and failure depend on how he performs his duties. To do all that is required of him, a tackle must have the speed of an end and the aggressiveness and all-round ability of a good back. It is needless to say that he must have courage, weight, strength and wonderful endurance to fulfil the requirements of his position.

The tackle's work on offense is indeed varied. When called behind the line he is used to lead the interference through the line, being, in reality, the "roadmaker" who plows clear the track along which the runner follows. On the plays around the end he leads the interference and is expected to prevent the opposing tackle and the defensive half back from stopping the play behind the line of scrimmage, thus giving the rest of the interference and the runner a chance to get out and beyond the opposing tackle. Then, again, he is called upon to take the full back or half back position to carry the ball through the line on a short cross-buck through or just outside the opposing tackle. The tackle is rarely used to run from his position in the line, as the play is a very poor one on a slippery, muddy field, such as is usually encountered in the month of November, when the important games are played. He may also be required to go over on the other side of his own line to take a position beside his own tackle, there to perform the duties of an end in boxing the opposing tackle, leaving the end whose place he has taken free to care for the defensive half back. The tackle's work when the point of attack is on his own side, inside or outside of him, requires that he shall block or box his opposing tackle long and successfully, until the play can be carried by.

It is very important that the tackle should have mastered the fundamental principles of blocking, breaking through, starting, carrying the ball and interfering, as given in a previous chapter. These principles he must have practiced until they have become a very part of his own make-up and can be performed practically without thought.

He and the end must learn to work together in boxing an opposing tackle or in opening holes through the opposing line. The tackle must always remember that he is responsible for the hole or opening between himself and his own guard. He must also remember that it is his duty to block the inside man of the opposing line, for often the opposing guard moves out very wide or one of the enemy's backs takes a position in the opposing line inside of tackle. This player then becomes the inside man and should be taken care of by the tackle, who should let his own end care for the opposing tackle.

A very important part of the tackle's work is on the defense, where he should exemplify everything that his name implies. He should tackle all the time and all over the field. He should break through and tackle behind the line, and should never be denied. He must not expect anyone else to make the tackle or stop the play. He must not let the runner get outside of his position, for that part of the field is protected only by the end.

The tackle must play low. If he is caught "up in the air" it is impossible for him to stop a hostile play short of a good gain. He must remember to play low, block low, charge low and tackle low. If the point of attack is directly at his position he must hit the interference not much above the knee. A mass play is not hard to stop if it is taken low. On the other hand it is almost impossible to stop if met by a tackler who stands erect.

The tackle should be an expert in the use of the stiff arm, so that he can keep the opposing tackle and end away from him and go through the line. The opposing end is the most dangerous man the tackle has before him, and this man should be carefully watched. The tackle must not in any circumstances permit himself to be boxed, and should nearly always break through the opposing line on the outside of his opponent. He should observe at the very outset of the game the methods which the opposing end and tackle use in blocking him, and, after taking in the situation thoroughly, he should adapt his style of play and mode of breaking through to the situation, so that he can frustrate the plans of his opponents. He and his defensive half back should have an understanding whereby they may sometimes shift positions just before the ball is put into play, thus enabling one or the other of them to get through and behind the opponents' line almost on the instant the play is started.

The tackle should watch the opposing backs very carefully, as he can often tell, by some movement or expression before the play is started, where it is to hit the line, and so be greatly helped in the endeavor to stop it. He must keep his eyes on the ball and break through the instant it is put into play, for it is much easier to break up a play before it is started, than after it has attained its full momentum. The tackle should never run behind his own line but should always go through the opponents' line, stopping the play from behind, if possible, and always watching out for criss-crosses, delayed passes and other trick plays. The tackle will not be easily fooled if he keeps his eyes on the ball. No forward should ever close his eyes in breaking through an opposing line or stopping a play.

When his own side is attempting a kick, the left tackle should leave his position and go straight down the field under the punt. He should go through on the inside of the defensive tackle, giving him a slight body check as he goes by. The tackle on the side of the kicker's leg must block longer but not too long, and should go down fast to stop the runner, in case he has not already been downed.

When the opposing side is going to kick, the two tackles should spread out on the line in the way that will best enable them to get through and block the kick. The tackle should take care and satisfy himself that the kick is not a fake, which may result in a play coming through the line inside of tackle or, more likely, since the full back may carry the ball on a direct pass beyond the line of scrimmage, around the end. The tackle should always go through hard and fast, using his hands to ward off the men protecting the kicker. He should then spring, with arms extended, high in the air in front of the kicker and try to block the kick, which he can often do. If he cannot block the kick, he can often compel the punter to kick almost straight up.

When a kick is blocked there is great opportunity for a touchdown. If the ball is bounding and can consequently be easily picked up, the tackle can frequently snatch it up and race on over the goal line. Sometimes he can kick the ball forward along the ground until it is kicked in goal, where he can fall on it for a touchdown.

The result of every game will depend largely on the strength of the two tackles. They are the men occupying the positions enabling them to stop all runs intended to go out beyond them, and they must be instrumental as well in stopping line plays. The tackle should use his head and should never be caught twice in the same manner by a trick of an opponent. He should be versatile and adapt himself to the situation.

"Be up and doing" should be the tackle's motto.

THE GUARD

Strength, weight and aggressiveness are as essential to a good guard as speed is to an end. A slow, lumbering guard is of no use; in fact, a slow man has no place in the game. Upon the center and the two guards depends the strength of the line and the strength here must be that of a stone wall, in order that the various offensive plays may be gotten well under way before the opponents can get through to break them up. The work that falls upon the guard calls for great exertion and instant action. The area of his play is limited, but if his position is attacked he must go through on the instant, as plays at that point in the line strike immediately.

When playing on the offensive, the guard must line up quickly, not more than a foot from his center—practically shoulder to shoulder. He should stand facing the opposing guard, ready to block him the instant the ball is put into play. He must never allow himself to be drawn out, for then the opposing center or defensive quarter back can break through. The guard should also play very low, as he cannot open holes in the line or do successful blocking when playing high.

After he has opened the hole, the guard can often help

the runner by pulling him along or by pushing him from behind, especially if the attack is on his side of the center. When the attack is on the center's opposite side, the guard should go through between the opposing guard and center, and block out the guard. Then, when he is through and behind the opposing line, he can cut off the opposing half back, part of the enemy's reinforcements, and, crossing over the center line, may possibly pull the runner along or interfere for him.

The guard is almost useless as a ground gainer, if used from his position. He may be called back behind the line, however, and used in the same way as a tackle, either for interference or for carrying the ball.

On defense the guard should play close to center, crouching low, facing the front, as this will be the direction from which the strong attack will come. The guard must not be drawn out too wide, although he is responsible for the hole between himself and tackle. He should be very effective in helping the center to stop all plays aimed at his position. He must never be caught "up in the air," for mass plays must be stopped from the bottom. The guard should always go through straight ahead, carrying the opposing guard back into the play or forcing him toward center, while he himself goes through instantly on the outside. He should go through on every play and never back off his own line. He should not wait and use his discretion about going through the line, for the attack of the opponents is too varied. Consequently, many of the plays seemingly meant for the opposite side of the line—and actually started in that direction—really strike at the position of the often-deceived guard.

When his side is kicking, the guard should play close to center and block long and effectively. He is practically in front of the kicker and, if he permits anyone to get through his position, the opponent will be directly in front of the kicker and will probably block his kick or interfere with the distance or the direction of the punt.

At the kick-off, after the kick, a guard should go down directly under the ball to prevent any return and to be on hand to line up instantly when the ball is downed. When the opponents are kicking, the guard is in one of the best positions to block kicks or to aid in getting the center or the other guard through for that purpose. The three center men should work together to get one of their number through. They can easily arrange a signal which will indicate what each one is to do and which one is to go through. With mutual assistance thus secured, one of the trio should go through almost instantly, as the defensive men have the free use of the hands and arms and so should be able to jerk open the opposing line. To illustrate, if the signal called for the center to go through, the left guard should pull his man to the left and the right guard can jerk the opposing center over to the right. At the same instant the center can assist by pushing the right guard to the left, with the left hand, using his right to open up the hole still further by pushing the opposing center further out of the way. This should open a road for the center to the punter. The man who goes through, if he does not block the kick, should hurry the punter so that he cannot get good distance or direction.

A guard should play upon the line of scrimmage, study his man, learn his methods and never be caught twice in the same way. Many of the methods of penetrating the opposing line will come to the guard who studies the situation. Too many players are machine-like in their methods. They are not versatile. They do not use their brains. The chief lesson for the football player to learn is the necessity for headwork.

THE CENTER

The center, like all the other members of a football team, should be active and fast on his feet and should above all things be strong and steady. No one but a man who is absolutely cool in all his work should attempt to play the important position of center. No play can start without first having the assistance of the center, and if he fails in any way the play will generally result in no gain or the loss of the ball. The center must follow the ball all the time; wherever the ball is, there the center must be also. No team can play a clean-cut, fast game if the center is slow.

The center's position for passing must depend largely upon his build and make-up. He should stand with one foot back and to the side of the other, judging the distance by his feeling of security on his feet. But his rear foot must not be too far back nor his feet too far apart. He must assume a good, strong position, ready to resist a charge from the front or a pull in the same direction.

The ball should be carefully passed with both hands. The movement should be more in the nature of a snap of the fingers and wrist, than a pass of the arms. The center must always remember not to change the direction or speed of his passes. A good motto to follow is:

"Not too hard, not too slow;
Not too high, not too low."

No quarter can handle irregular passing without mistakes. Many of the fumbles made by the quarter are due to the unsteadiness of the center. Under the present rules the work of the center in passing has been much extended by the addition of the direct pass to the half, quarter or full back for a run around tackle or end. Hence the center must be very proficient in his passing to make all these plays go off smoothly. The ball should go back accurately or there will be fumbles and delays.

On all offensive plays, the center knows on which side of the line the attack is to be made and should go through between the opposing center and the play. After he has gotten through he can block off part of the opponents' secondary line of defense and assist the runner by pulling, pushing or giving him additional interference.

On defense, the work of the center is very important and varied. He should do almost as much tackling as the defensive quarter back, especially if the line is attacked between the two tackles. His position on the defense is a much freer one than that of either guard. He can shift his position from in front to either side of the opposing center, being careful, however, to work always with the offensive quarter. There is no one who is in a better position to size up the opponents' play before it is started than the center. He should watch the ball all the time and, simultaneously, the opposing backs. He should play close to his man and charge him hard with both hands, arms stiff, the instant the ball is put into play. As has been said, no lineman should ever be caught "up in the air," but should always play low and charge low. He should work with his guard in breaking through the line.

After he has charged his man the center should go wherever the play leads him. If he is on the defensive and the play is not at his position, he should go back of his own line and stop the runner. He can often do this even when the play is far out towards the end.

The center must be very careful in his pass to the full

back for a kick. He should practice different ways of passing, finally choosing that plan which gives the quickest and truest results. After the pass he should protect the kicker, then go down under the punt, directly under the ball. When the opponents punt, the center, working with the two guards, should break through and block the kick. The center and the guards may allow the quarter to break through, but this is hardly advisable, since the opposing full back may run with the ball on a direct pass. It is better for the quarter to drop back from three to five yards behind his center, to watch out for "fake kicks" around the end or through the line. If the opposing center is a dangerous man, when going down under punts the defensive center should charge him back to prevent him from going down the field and making costly tackles.

THE HALF BACKS

The position of half back is one that is hard to fill. The half backs, together with the full back, are expected to be the standard ground gainers of the eleven. The half back is called upon to make fierce plunges into the line and rapid dashes around the end. Hence great care should be used in the selection of men to fill the half back positions. They should be chosen for speed, grit and endurance. Each should have a quick eye and the ability to act on the instant as the situation demands. The hole in the opposing line will not always be where it is expected and the interference will not always be as desired. The half back should use his eyes constantly, to take advantage of any opening or hurdle anyone who may fall under the interference, thereby becoming a "dead one."

It should be decided at the very first which half back position the candidate is to fill, for, while the general duties

of the two half backs are practically the same, the plays
are in opposite directions. The position for the half back
to assume on the defensive depends on the style of game
that the team is playing. There is little left of the old
formation of three backs in a row. Several of the latest
formations and the positions of the half backs in these are
shown in the chapter on "Offense." All of the back field
men should exercise great care in taking the same positions of foot, body, hand and eye in all the formations.
They should not, by word or by act, give away the point
of attack or the direction in which the play is going. This
is very important, yet many good backs are guilty of such
offenses.

In bucking the line, the half back should go in low and
hard. This does not mean that he should carry his head
so low that he cannot see where he is going; the body must
be carried low without having the head bent down. If the
back does not use his eyes he is just as likely to run into
one of his own men or into the arms of an opponent as into
the opening. In line smashing, the back should carry the
ball against the pit of the stomach. He should hold it securely with both arms, for he need not use either hand to
ward off interference, as this would be useless in straight
line smashing. He should by all means keep his feet, so
that his team mates can help him along, and he must not
be thrown toward his own goal; he and his helpers must
prevent this. On all plays around the end or just outside
of tackle the half back should carry the ball under his outside arm; he will then have the other arm free to keep off
the opposing tacklers. Very few half backs make use of
this important feature of their work. No back should ever
run toward his own goal; his duty is to gain ground, not
to lose that already made.

Carrying the ball is not more than one-third of the work required of a half back on the offensive. The half back must work just as hard and conscientiously when the other men on the team have the ball. He is then required to go into the interference and "clear the track" of opposing tacklers, or to aid in pushing or pulling the runner along for an extra yard on plunges through the line.

The defensive work of the half back depends largely upon the style of attack used by the opponents, but all backfield men should, if possible, be able to kick, be sure tacklers and be proficient in the handling of punts. The directions in these features of his game are given elsewhere under their respective heads.

THE QUARTER BACK

What the general is to the army, the quarter back is to the football team. He directs the battle and success, in a large measure, depends on his plan of campaign. He must be a man of the highest mental and physical qualities. He must be a man who can inspire confidence in the mind of every player on his eleven. Mentally, he must be of quick thought and judgment and must have plenty of nerve. Physically, the quarter back must have strength and clean activity and, above all, an unlimited amount of endurance.

The necessity for these qualifications in a good quarter back will be easily seen by a review of his duties given under the head of "Generalship."

When playing on the offensive, the quarter back should stand just far enough behind the center to be able to touch the latter with his finger tips. The quarter back should always face the center. His feet should be planted squarely under him and just far enough apart to ensure steadiness. He should, with the center, be the first of the team to get into position before a play.

The quarter back should always give the signals, because he is in the best position to know the condition of his own men, can most readily discover the strength and weakness of the opponents and can save time and error by himself calling the signals of the plays, which he alone can start. The quarter back should be the practical captain on the field and should be unhampered in his work by anyone. The captain may consult him when time is out but the working should be such that consultation is unnecessary at any other time.

The quarter back should be thoroughly familiar with his list of plays and should also know under what conditions each play can be used to the best advantage. He should know when to order a kick and when a rush. He must distribute the work of his team among his men in such a way that every man is ready for more. The best and strongest player may be overworked by an injudicious quarter and, as a result, this player may fail when his best services are most needed to win success for the team.

To make himself sure in receiving the ball from the center, the quarter should practice as much as possible with the center. In case of a fumble, the quarter should always fall on the ball immediately. In passing the ball to the runner he must be very accurate and swift. In runs outside of tackle, the ball should be passed to the runner as soon as the quarter can get it out of his hands. The ball should be passed ahead of the runner, making him come up to it, but it must always be tossed accurately and safely, so that the runner need lose no time trying to get it. In plays through the line between tackles the ball should be placed against the stomach of the runner as he comes by the quarter, and the latter should then help the runner to break through.

Showing how to hurdle the line.

In starting a play the quarter should be very careful not to give away to his opponents the intended point of attack.

Under the present rules the quarter back is a most valuable offensive player, since he can himself carry the ball on a direct pass from the center, provided he crosses the scrimmage line five yards from the point where the ball was in play. But even when he does not carry the ball, his place as an aid to the runner is most important. In plays going between the tackles, the quarter is in position to help the runner by pulling him along after he is tackled, by holding him up or pushing him through. In plays through outside the tackle, the quarter should be in the interference ahead of the runner. After a play is started the quarter need not watch for fumbles, as the following end is a general safety man.

The qualifications necessary for a good offensive quarter are usually found in a man weighing between 150 and 170 pounds. Hence, on the defensive, the quarter back and the full back usually change positions, for the light-weight quarter cannot readily stop the mass plays, but should be very good in open field tackling and handling punts. Whoever plays quarter on the defensive should be very alert in watching opponents for the direction of their plays. He should always keep his men watchful and active in breaking up the attack of the opposing team. He should watch for "fake" plays, call out to his men where the attack is to come, and keep them on tip-toe, ready to smash up the coming charge.

The quarter back must be the leader of the team when it is in action. He must do his own work coolly accurately and swiftly, and at the same time do all that he can to keep his men up to the fighting pitch. He must be a director, a fighter and a good talker.

THE FULL BACK

The duties of the full back on the offensive are largely the same as those of the half back. The full back, however, on account of his position midway between the half backs and directly back of the center, is better situated for line plunging than for runs around the ends, and it is here that he is usually called upon to advance the ball.

The full back is the battering ram of the eleven. He it is who is commonly the man projected into the mass of players in the center, and a player must have 'rugged endurance and ability to withstand the hard usage incumbent on a man who plays this position well and conscientiously. The full back is also often used in the interference, of which he is a member on practically every play when he is not carrying the ball. He must be strong, heavy and full of courage, ready to go up against the opposing line with an abandon that would be in evidence were there no line there at all. The important part which he has to perform in every play makes it imperative that he be a man of iron endurance and in perfect physical trim.

The full back must also be a good kicker or else able to take the place of the man who does the kicking, when the time comes for such a play. The kicking must be done from the full back's position, and, if the regular occupant of the position does not do it, the full back should be able to take some other position to assist in strengthening the defense, weakened by the withdrawing of the kicker from his regular position.

On defense the full back is the final obstacle in the path of the enemy. He must guard his own goal, ready to tackle any hostile runner who has succeeded in evading the men in front of him. To do this he should assume a position 15 yards or so back of the line of scrimmage, following the plays from side to side and holding himself in readiness to get into the path of any runner who may break through.

The defensive full back must also be a man able to handle punts sent by the opponents. He must be a sure catcher and able to run back with the ball through an open field.

THE TACKLING DUMMY

A reference to the accompanying diagram will give a good general idea of the essentials in the construction of a serviceable tackling dummy. Three solid posts 15 feet in length, the cross piece mortised into the other two, which are sunk at least three feet in the ground, will provide the general framework, while a swivel pulley in the middle and a straight pulley mortised into one of the side pieces provide the tackle for the rope from which the dummy hangs. The dummy itself can be constructed of duck or heavy canvas, stuffed with excelsior or sawdust. No weight is needed to counter-balance the weight of the dummy, as the rope can be made long enough to permit its being held by a man at the other end.

The dummy should be held about six inches off the ground, and the rope should be long enough to allow its being paid out as the player makes the tackle.

The practice dive at the dummy should be varied in length. The long dive which is often necessary in a real game should be taken straight from the spring, not up in the air and then down at the dummy as many players will try to make it at first. The short dives should be made with such force that the dummy will be carried back in the player's arms for a considerable distance at the finish.

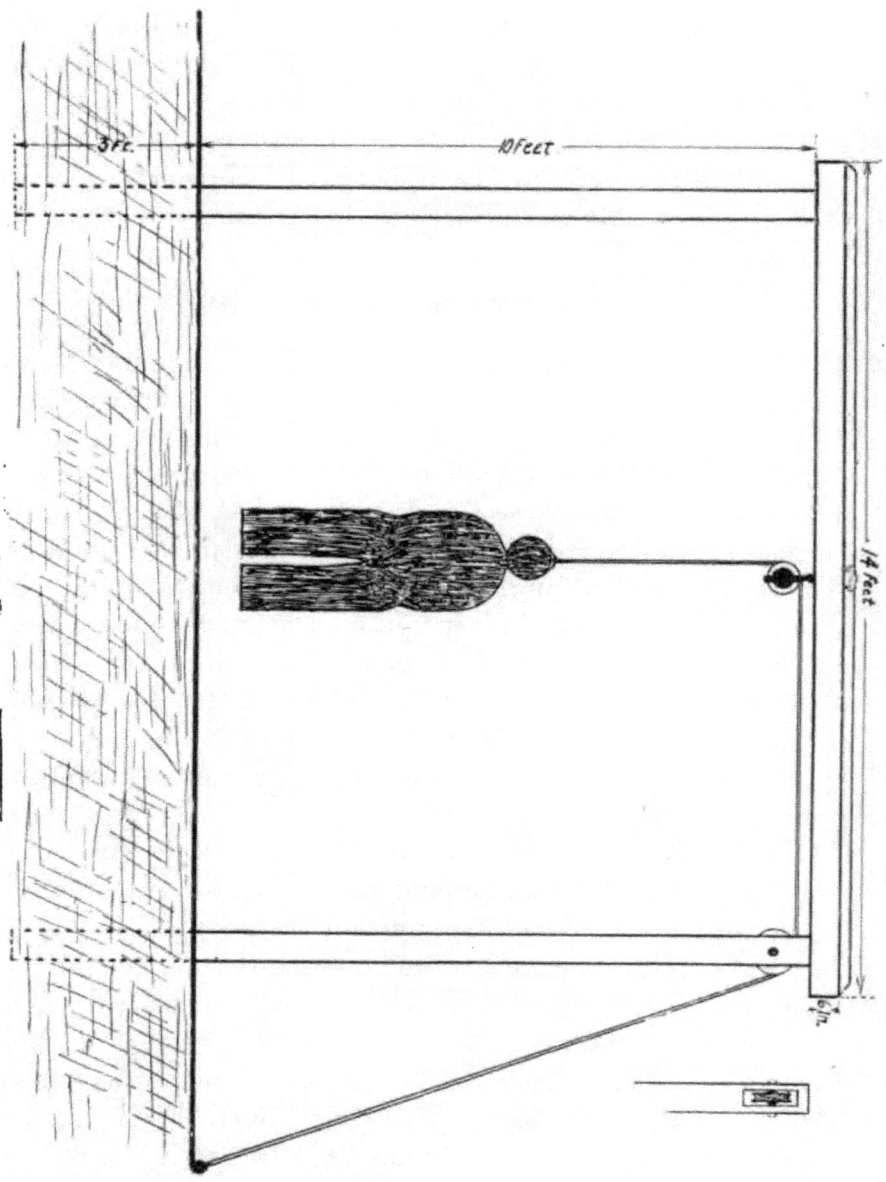

A tackling dummy similar to this can easily be provided for every football field. Do not do without it.

The dummy can also be used in practice on offensive play, the candidates for the eleven being given work in warding and interfering. In this the rope should be held fast while the players go into the dummy low and hard with the shoulder or hip striking it. Flying dives, which form a spectacular and at times effective sort of inter-ference, can also be practiced in this way. In all this offensive work players should be taught to avoid the use of their hands on the dummy.

The ground on which the players alight after making the tackle should be covered with straw, sawdust or some other sort of padding early in the season, although later on, when the men have become hardened to their work, the ground may be left in its natural state.

The tackling dummy should form a part of the train-ing equipment of every team. It is inexpensive, takes up no room necessary for any other purpose and its benefits are great. Another advantage of the machine is the fact that it can be used for practice by a very small squad, which can be coached in both defensive and offensive tactics.

THE CHARGING MACHINE

A practical charging machine is a very important ad-dition to the training camp of any football team, and the expense connected with its construction is by no means great. The accompanying photograph shows the sim-plicity of the device, which can be built by any average mechanic. The weight of the machine need not be great, as a player or two from the squad can be used as additional ballast when the need for weight is felt. This will, how-ever, be necessary only when the entire line is charging the machine, for squads of even two or three can use the machine to advantage.

The position linemen should assume just before the ball is snapped—head and eyes up, hips down.

The charging machine develops speed in starting with the snap of the ball, a virtue which greatly strengthens the offense of any team. Its main value, however, rests in its use for the cultivation of form on defense. In this case the charging machine represents the opponents on offense, and one of the men standing on the machine the opposing center. The line forms as if in actual play and, the moment the ball is snapped by the man on the machine, the players charge together, arms straight out and stiff, eyes to the front. This cultivates the players in the use of their arms in breaking through an offensive line, and prevents that common fault of going in with head down. The arms must be kept out stiff or the player's head will strike the machine. He must also keep his head up, in order to strike the machine in the right place with his hands. The work also strengthens the legs, arms and backs of the players, providing many of the benefits of actual scrimmage without any of its dangers.

One of the pronounced benefits of a charging machine is the fact that it also gives the coach or trainer an excellent opportunity of securing data regarding the relative speed of his candidates in charging. A player who is behind the rest can be picked out with ease and placed side by side with a faster man for the purpose of cultivating his speed. In this way a line can be taught to charge together and with speed, to keep low, to use the hands in getting through an offensive line and to cultivate form in general.

One consideration that should not be lost sight of in the construction of a charging machine is the height of the pad against which the players charge. This should be placed low, and especial care should be taken in this respect, as a large share of the benefits that might be derived from the use of the machine will be nullified if the players rise as they strike the device.

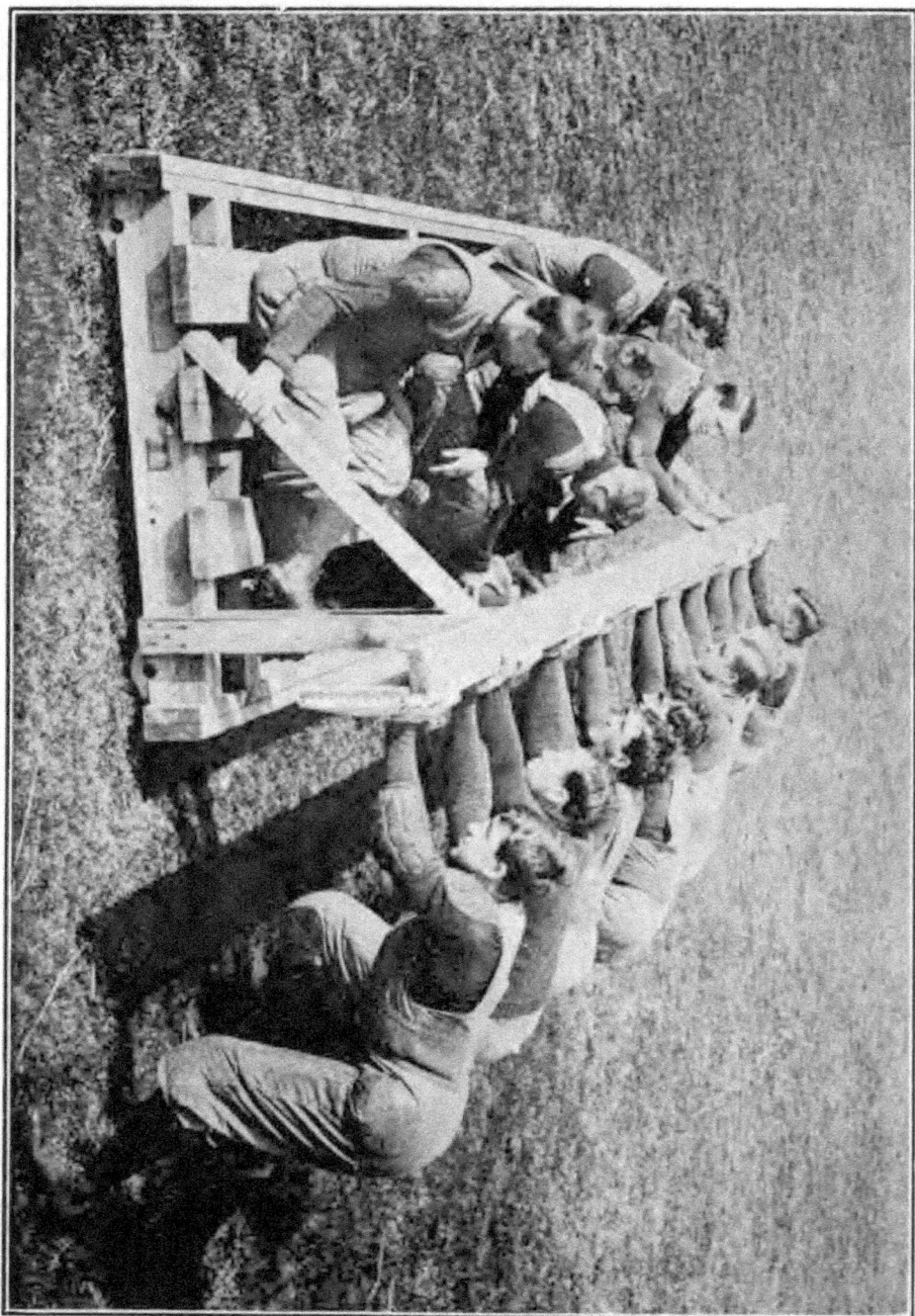

TRAINING

The training and conditioning of the contestants for the football team are matters of primary importance to the success of the team in its games. The men owe it to themselves to get into good condition, and the trainer cannot exercise too great care in getting the players ready for the struggles ahead.

The days have passed in which men were required to go to extremes in training. The era of half-cooked beefsteak is no more. In fact, the proper training of the men requires no more restrictions, so far as diet is concerned, than anyone who desires to be the possessor of a good, healthy, normal body should observe. The men who present themselves as candidates for a football team are generally of good, moral habits, and are not broken down by excesses of any kind. They have not abused nature, and take training easily.

The worry and nervous strain incident to the training are matters which should be watched more closely than anything else. This is especially true of men who are new to the game, but most of all are these troubles apt to develop in the quarter back and captain, through the many responsibilities thrust upon them. The amount of hard work, of the sort which might possibly injure a player before he is in proper condition, should be minimized as far as is in the power of the trainer. In fact, during the very first part of the season nothing of the kind should be attempted. As the season progresses, work of this character should be along the lines of gradual development. Nor is the physical side of training the only one. It is equally important that the mental training should be watched and just as carefully developed.

EARLY SEASON'S WORK To begin with, the coach, trainer and captain will face a mass of material of different physical characteristics. The varying ages of the men must be taken into consideration in the kind and amount of work necessary in their proper preparation for the game. The same work cannot be laid out for the rapidly growing freshman as for the fully developed senior who has played perhaps his four years on the team. The needs of the different individuals must be suited.

Commence with the more simple fundamentals, such as starting, passing and a little kicking. Be careful to avoid too much kicking of the ball while the men's muscles are soft, as it is very easy to develop that muscular ailment popularly known as "Charley horse" in the kicking leg. and this will not only retard the progress of the individual for the time but may prevent him from doing his best work in any game through the entire season. To be a good player a man must have a good pair of legs, and care must be taken of them.

The men must start with the beginning of the season to give up drinking water during the practice or in games. It is no detriment during a hard game to rinse out the mouth with water, but this rule of giving it up as a drink, on the field of play, should be followed all through the season.

It is almost unnecessary to add that the duration of practice time should be short at the beginning and gradually increased as the season advances.

LATER WORK As the season progresses the amount of work to be given must be adapted to the different requirements of the players with increasing care. No two men can be worked successfully on the same plan. It is a very common mistake to attempt to train everyone in the same manner and by the same amount of work. The characteristics of each individual should furnish the data for the trainer's allotment of work.

Throughout the season the men must all, however, have plenty of work and experience at playing the game; yet it is useless to practice after the men are tired and exhausted and have lost their "ginger."

Late in the season care should be taken that no player becomes over-trained. The day before each hard game should be spent in putting on the final touches and toning up the men. Light work only should be attempted at this time and it is better to have no scrimmage practice at all. A man who enters the game full of energy and go will be of far greater value than one who is lame and wearied by work of this kind at this late day. The slight benefit to his mechanical proficiency, derived from this eleventh-hour scrimmage work, is more than counter-balanced by the player's consequent lack of spirit and tone.

REGULARITY The hour of starting practice should be the same all through the season. Do not have practice too soon after the meal time. Work must be exacted in all kinds of weather, as the day of the game may be just as bad as the practice afternoon, and the game must be played. The work will not hurt the men and they will become accustomed to playing in all kinds of weather. Care should be taken on bad days, however, that players do not get too warm, only to stand around and cool off quickly. Blankets or sweaters should be thrown around the men when they are not working.

The meal hours should be regular and all the men should be present at the same time. This is a rule, the breaking of which should not be tolerated for an instant. The same regularity should be observed in the hour at which the men retire at night and rise in the morning. Plenty of sleep is needed. The player should be methodical in all his habits. The men must not be permitted to smoke or use alcohol in any form.

CLEANLINESS Cleanliness is important to the health of anyone. The conditions in which football is played demand that every man take a bath after every practice is over. A good shower bath is the best and can be easily arranged. A long, hot bath should never be taken, as it is weakening. A good rub with a coarse towel after the bath, followed by the training massage, will be of great aid to the men in getting into condition. The player's physical condition will be reflected in his high spirits after the day's work is over.

INJURIES Serious injuries should be attended to by a surgeon at once. A football player is as susceptible to injury as is any other well conditioned athlete, and his period of convalescence will be just as long. Prompt attention will save many days in the period of recuperation.

It is also important that the minor injuries be carefully looked after by the trainer or coach, or they may result in more serious conditions. Recovery from small sprains and bruises can be facilitated by the application of hot towels, and this should be attended to immediately. Sprains can be protected by proper bandages.

CLOTHING AND PROTECTION The players should be provided with proper clothing for the game. Special padding is often necessary for some men. This is especially true when there is a liability to injury in a weak knee or a weak collar bone. The wearing of clothes padded in a proper manner will prevent many injuries which, while they may be trivial, would nevertheless retard the work of the player.

The shoes must be kept well cleated, as the player should have a good footing. Nose guards are a source of annoyance and should not be worn.

TRAINING TABLE A training table should be provided for all the regulars and substitutes. The men are brought together through its influence and there are regular meal hours for all. The food of the men should be looked after closely by the trainer or coach. The modern training table should be an attractive place to the players. Thus they become anxious to be there, because of the plain, wholesome, well-cocked foods to be had. The training table should be the best place to board in the whole town. The bill of fare should be changed often, so that there will be no monotony. Pork, sweet-breads or pie should not be served. Coffee and tea must be given up. Nothing that has been prepared by frying should be found at the training table. What an array of good things is left!

THE MENTAL TRAINING The mental training of the candidates for the football team is as important as the cultivation of the physical side of the men. This must not be neglected, although it is often completely lost sight of. There should be some especial drill for those who learn slowly. The coach and trainer will be called upon to devise many different ways to impress certain facts on the different individuals. Each man will be impressed in a different manner. No two men can be told in exactly the same way with the desired result. The players must improve each day in their knowledge of the game, for at most there are but about ten weeks to learn the lessons that must be taught, and the time is too short for a leisurely course.

DEVELOPMENT OF THE TEAM

The first requisite to the development of a football team is a study of the entire season's campaign. The successful working plan of former elevens is not a safe rule in the preparation of a new team. Although the games may be played against the same old opponents, an entirely new set of problems will be presented for the coach to solve. These problems may spring up in the gradation of games on the schedule or in changes in the class or coaches of the rival elevens, but the main problem is one of men. The coach must not only know the physical abilities of his players, but he must divine early in the season the character and traits of the men whom he will have to trust with important positions when the strain of late-season games taxes strength and training to their limits and calls out the reserve forces of grit, original head work and moral stamina.

Even in the mere mechanical drills, both the amount and kind of work depend upon the individual player. It is unimportant whether any such thing as a team appears on the football field during the early practice. In fact, too much attention to team work too early in the season may ruin the opportunities to develop a good team later. If the coach or trainer will spend his entire time preparing each man, as a mechanic finishes up the separate parts of his creation before putting it together, the various positions can be fitted into each other in a short time, to make a smoothly running, accurate and strong football machine.

In preparing these cogs of the football mechanism it is proper to have ideals, yet the materials offered for the construction of a football team are never all that are desired and, as for ideals, seldom does even a single candidate on an entire team come up to the mark set in the coach's mind. There is constant danger that the existence in the mind of the coach of an ideal team may actually injure the eleven in actual process of development. To escape this difficulty the coach must continually remind himself of conditions, not fancies, and make the best possible out of the material at hand. One means to attain this end is the constant habit of taking an inventory of the men. A study of abilities and weaknesses that develop from day to day, and the observation of peculiarities in build and temperament will quickly show how players can be better fitted into the team where their muscles and brains will count most in making it stronger. Very likely the final assignment of positions may not be the ones which the coach would best like to see the men playing, yet it makes a stronger machine.

It is not the amount of football knowledge a player may have, but rather how much of the theory he possesses that can be put into practice, that wins games.

If the practice is not interesting enough to burn an indelible impression of every rudiment of football into the player's working knowledge, it is wasted. The coach can best instruct his men by putting on his football suit and illustrating exactly what he wants done, not only in fundamentals, but in team play. Confidence of the members of the team, one in the other, and constant interest in how each comrade is developing will in time form a team spirit, a factor quite as potent in carrying a pig-skin as an extra hundred pounds of muscle. The main requirement all the time is work—hard work—not the bruising kind, either, but such as develops and quickens the men. Along with this ambition to work, the player must have a goal, some such aim, for example, as to repeat each play a thousand times in patient, daily practice, and never to repeat it,—no matter how old a story the play may become to him,—without doing better than before. Half-hearted repetitions are useless in football.

THE FIRST WEEK TO TEN DAYS

The time for the preparation of the individual parts of the team is the first week or ten days of training. Persistence and patience ought to show the general abilities of the men in this period and enable the coach to select very nearly the places they can play on the team. The earlier the choice of a team can be made, the greater will be its perfection in the season's height. This preparation period ought to be free from any work such as regular scrimmage, in which the men may be injured. To get into fair condition should be the first general aim. Passing the ball. starting, kicking, catching and the work in squads of four, together with other work given under "Rudiments" in this book, will develop and harden players till their first scrimmage is without danger. Still, even this same easy-going program of daily drills, unless carefully watched, can be pushed beyond the limits of the best team's endurance. The distribution of preliminary work is very like the plan of campaign—a matter of discovering the needs of the individual. It is especially advisable to keep men who are slow on their feet working hard at starting practice and those who handle passes poorly busy at kicking and punting.

PRACTICE IN KICKING

The first two weeks of the season, before the stress of the real work begins, give a golden opportunity to discover invaluable punters, place kickers and goal kickers. The best way is to use, for a few days, the American idea of an equal opportunity to everyone. The most likely candidates, no matter how superficially unpromising some of them really appear, should then be selected for special kicking practice daily. Sometimes the best kicker develops where such ability was least expected. He may even be a veteran who has played seasons without discovering the power in his kicking toe. Great care is necessary that these men do not work too long. The early practice is designed entirely to learn form, for this quality, so hard to define because it is the most difficult part of kicking, is the key to both distance and accurate direction.

As soon as the good kickers begin to forge ahead, practice should be concentrated into kicking from behind a scrimmage line, where all this work is done in the game. Men who can kick 70 yards in the open often cannot punt 50 consistently while facing the charge of an opposing line. Not merely one, but three or four good men, should be developed in the punting department.

There is still another indispensable set of kickers, who need not necessarily be on the punting squad. They are the place-kickers. A drop kick or one from placement from the field may be the deciding factor in the important game of the season. On the majority of football teams the best place kicker will not be a good punter, for usually the large men make the best place kicks. Also, they are likely to be in the best condition after the exhausting work required to make a touchdown and therefore, having steadier nerves and muscles than light men, are more accurate. Furthermore, a tall, heavy man makes his goal by the sheer weight behind the swing of his leg and is not compelled, like his lighter comrade, to disturb his aim by the hard swing of his toe against the ball.

INDIVIDUAL DRILLS

To fill in every spare nook and cranny of the time between the different periods of team instruction with drills which perefect the individual is not only a time-saving policy, but may often result in altering the fortunes of battle on some hard-fought field later on. One such drill which men must practice by themselves is the art of falling on or around the ball. An accurate style of launching the body at the ball, while it rolls on the ground, and of pinning it fast, will save many a fumble from becoming more serious when the time comes for the actual competition. The ends especially need to know this branch of the diving art. Every man on the squad has a few spare minutes which he can devote to this work under the eye of an assistant coach. These few minutes, if faithfully used throughout the season, will make the men proficient in a trick which requires infallible judgment of the eye and a quick leap. Work with the tackling dummy can be done in the same manner, although the dummy teaches no more than the form of a dive, while the effectiveness which makes the players a stone wall on defense can be learned only by tackling live, dodging runners. A particularly important phase of the tackling is daily work in sending the team down the field under punts.

A group which requires small groups of players at a time is the charging machine. From five to ten minutes of this work daily, especially with the forwards, will effectually strengthen the straight-arm work of the linesmen, and will quicken the slow men until the entire line springs into action as one player.

FORMATIONS OF FOURS

In the early season, before such a thing as a team exists, its place can be, to a great extent, filled by a division of all the material into squads of four. These are little, rudimentary teams consisting of a center, quarter back and two halves. All the men who appear fitted for center can play the position on these squads and the quarter back material can pass the ball. Every other position on the team will fit into the half back work of these squads of four. Of course, in this formation, the center learns just how to stand, how to pass the ball to the quarter and how to charge when passing it. It is also obvious that the quarter backs, especially if there are several likely candidates, could receive no better work. The three other men line up so quickly that the quarter back's practice is nearly doubled, while he can reel off signals for all ordinary plays until he is able to think far faster than an entire eleven could execute his commands. He can use these backs for imaginary plunges through the line, as well as for runs around the end.

But a still greater value of the squads of four is the benefit to the linesmen. In many a season which starts with doubtful prospect, the winning shake-up which gives the coach the title of "Wizard" is nothing more than the application of the half back lessons, taught through the squad of four. The guards, tackles and ends receive as much benefit from playing the half back positions as the regular halves, for, first of all, this work increases the speed of every man. It is often good policy to place a fast and slow man together on a squad, where, instead of retarding the speed of the fast man, the slow player develops as much ginger as his speedier companion. Wind and endurance, which fit men for the strenuous work later on and which may even be the foundation for producing the fastest

Work for the center, quarter back and all the other men. This work will develop speed, endurance and starting. All will become familiar with handling and carrying the ball.

eleven of the season, are certain products of this squad drill. The team which is picked from such preliminary formations has an entire set of linesmen, familiar with the duties of the back field positions.

The inevitable result of placing men with such training on the line is to give the offense great variety of attack. Whenever these same linesmen, later in the season, are called back to carry the ball, they are at home. They know what to do and exactly how it should be done. These linesmen will thus be enabled to take their share of the offensive work off the shoulders of the backs, who, in many elevens, are required to do more than any man's strength can endure. Many linesmen will prove to be ground-gainers of the highest ability and effectiveness. Frequently the men playing in the line, though they may have been tried out, have not sufficient practice in ground-gaining tactics to become successes, whereas, had they received one-half the opportunity of the backs in practice of advancing the ball, they would develop into offensive players even more valuable than the regular occupants of the backfield positions.

Even after linesmen prove to be of little use as ground-gainers, as some of them undoubtedly will, their training behind the scrimmage line will be of wonderful value in the performance of their regular duties.

SIGNAL WORK

The drill which makes an effective unit out of an eleven; which enables it to strike fast and hard, time after time, as one man; in short, the making of the football machine, is signal practice. To start together and stay together is the first law of this drill. The plays here are run off much faster than in any game, since there is no necessity of waiting for the lining up of a defensive team. The

Trying out and developing men for the back field positions. Linemen and in fact all the candidates will be greatly benefited by this work.

men learn to fall instantly into their proper places, to shift with mechanical precision at the quarter back's command, and when, by this process, enough plays have been graven on their minds, they will learn new formations as if by instinct.

Two or three plays a day will not be too many. The rule of "hurry" must be universally applied. The slowest man must realize that he is holding back the play until he is in place and ready for action. Substitutes must be as thoroughly trained as the regulars in the positions they are expected to fill, for the entire eleven is no faster than its slowest member. The speed developed by the signal practice is speed both of action and of thought. Without one of these qualities the possession of the other is a useless asset.

INDIVIDUAL POSITIONS

The work of each man in playing his position is shown in the chapters on Offense and Defense. As the season progresses, each individual should be studied, not only to discover his capabilities in his own position but to teach .where, on certain shifts of the play, he can be used to best benefit the team as a whole. Sometimes it is best for the team that an offensive half back should play a defensive end, while the offensive end plays defensive quarter, half back or perhaps defensive full back. This study of individuals will help make a team uniformly strong. Especially on defense will it strengthen the weak points, which, if not fortified, the opponents will be sure to discover.

OFFENSE

An offense can be finished only by scrimmage work. As early as the men are able to stand it, about one-quarter of each day's work ought to be devoted to scrimmage practice. The first two weeks of formation and signal drills are sufficient to put the men into condition for the rough wear of scrimmage. In completing an offense the coach must not only give every man on the team a thorough preliminary drill in offensive tactics, but, if he hopes for a strong, varied attack, he must allow each man a thorough trial in carrying the ball during actual scrimmages.

No rules can be laid down for building up an offense. The attack will never be alike in any two years, unless the very same men compose the team. The peculiarities of the men will determine how the attack should be arranged. Games cannot be won without a strong, consistent offense, yet the time devoted to its development will be comparatively little in some years, while in others it will remain the all-important problem up to the very end of the season. It is poor policy to interrupt the work of two scrimmaging elevens solely to correct individual faults. Remember these lessons and impress them upon the football candidate at some other time.

DEFENSE

Too.often the time devoted to defense during a season is all too short. Frequently teams do not have a full second eleven on the gridiron and in many colleges there is never a complete reserve team at any time during the year. But, even without stopping the rushes of an offensive eleven, much can be learned in drills at tackling, charging and breaking through. When a full quota is not available, these drills can be made quite thorough by the use of smaller opposing squads, corresponding very nearly to the squad of four formations. A special defensive drill for kicks, punts and blocking place kicks should occupy at least a quarter of each day's practice. In the defensive instruction, as on offense, the faults of the individuals, in nearly all

instances, are best corrected in private, either after the
practice or early next day.

ASSISTANTS

"Too many cocks spoil the broth" in football as in any
other realm of endeavor, and the problem of assistant
coaches is a very serious matter. Assistants are invaluable
if rightly used, but if they are not they will ruin the best
team. The one principle never to be forgotten in
portioning out the assistant's work is that no player shall
have the style of his coaching changed during the season.
The assistants should never be permitted to coach the regulars. One man ought to have complete charge of that,
or, if a staff of coaches has the regular team in hand, then
the work should be so divided that the man who coaches
the forwards has entire charge of the linesmen; the head
coach of the ends should be absolute in his position, and
the opinion of the coach for the backs should be final in
his department.

Early in the season the coach should study and decide
on the best style for coaching each player, and then stick
to it.

It is well to have the assistant coach keep the reserve
team in shape for scrimmage with the regulars, for the
individualities of his coaching will make the plays of his
eleven a little different from that of the first team and will
furnish the regulars, in a measure, an opponent whose style
they do not know, which they must solve while in action.
Some of the very best assistants are veteran players who
are either still in college or are residents of the college town.

THE EVENING'S WORK

How often do we see a team continually making the same mistakes in game after game! Mistakes in generalship, mistakes in the work of the individuals show themselves with a frequency that is almost inexplicable.

Often the apportionment of the work among the individuals has been poorly done and advantage has not been taken in the games of the opportunities given under the rules, such as carrying the ball out of bounds when being downed near the sideline, or touching the ball as it is about to roll out of bounds on a punt and making the opponents take it for scrimmage within a yard of the sideline, instead of being permitted to carry it in for 15 yards. Many other instances could be noted in which similar cases of poor teaching crop out in the work of an eleven.

To remedy such faults should be the earnest aim of the coach, and he should lose no opportunity.

All or nearly all the schools and colleges which support football teams have a training table where the players assemble at meal time. Every evening after dinner is finished at least 30 minutes should be spent in conversation that has a direct bearing on the preparation of the men for their duties in the field. This time is usually wasted if the players leave training quarters immediately after the meal is finished. It can be made of much benefit to the men, however, and at the same time will not interfere to any appreciable extent with their study hours.

It is well that the work of each evening be systematized. The great benefit to be derived from what is advised in this chapter is that the players themselves are required to do much of the thinking. In thinking over the game with the idea of criticising it, the men will be much impressed and better prepared for the future.

MONDAY

On Monday evening the coach should require each of the men at the training quarters to present two written criticisms of the game played the Saturday before, the statements to bring out the mistakes that were made and the remedies which should be applied in particular instances.

The field for review should consist of the mistakes made by the individuals, the mistakes in team play and the manner and spirit in which the game was played. Opportunities lost when particular conditions presented themselves in the game, and the failure of the team to properly benefit by the mistakes of the opponents and their weaknesses can thus be indelibly impressed on the minds of the football pupils.

The coach or trainer can read these suggestions and comment on their correctness or fallacy. Also he may add to the criticisms other good and helpful suggestions and urge all to avoid in the future the mistakes mentioned. It is one of the most practical lessons possible, outside of the actual game itself, that can be brought to the attention of the player.

The rules are generalizations which must be mastered, but queer conditions arise in every game, and no book has ever been written which covers these varied circumstances. Furthermore, no book can be written which will be able to state just what will come up through the progress of a game.

It is in correcting the mistakes of the past that hopes rest for a better future, and the Monday evening half-hour can be made one of great profit. It is, as well, a half-hour of actual pleasure to the earnest football player.

TUESDAY

Every training quarters should be equipped with a blackboard. It is easy to have regular gridiron lines painted on the board, which can be used to advantage to illustrate plays and to discuss the problems that present themselves for solution in the different parts of the field.

Ideal situations may be presented or complicated conditions marked out, and the player can be tested in the facility with which he grasps the imaginary plays, as well as the accuracy with which he solves the problems thus presented. Football makes players think, and the blackboard affords a method more realistic than mere dreamy questionings. It lends interest to the general work, especially during the player's early experience.

The work having been arranged beforehand, only 15 or 20 minutes will be required for the actual blackboard illustrations and the balance of the time can be spent in singing, talking and joking.

WEDNESDAY

The average football player is lacking in accurate knowledge of the football rules. It is very important that every man should know the rules and know them instantly. The opportunity to take advantage of them on the field of play will not last always. The player does not often have time to hesitate.

There is no better way for the men to gain a proper knowledge of the rules than by instituting a quiz on them at least once a week. The players themselves should each be required to present two questions on the rules every Wednesday evening. These questions should be signed and read at the Wednesday evening meeting.

Rules are nothing but football laws which must be

obeyed. The practitioner in court who can quickly interpret a law bearing on the case that is being tried has an instant advantage over his slower opponent who is, for the moment, mystified. Correspondingly, no man can be a great football player unless he is an adept at the rules of the game.

Urge the men at the next "Rule Quiz" to bring out some new feature under the rules. The player, in looking up and preparing these questions, will become thoroughly conversant with all the rules. This, together with what each man brings out at the weekly conference, should leave nothing unnoticed, down to the obscurest section of the laws that govern the game.

THURSDAY

On Thursday evening especial attention can be given to the work of the captain and quarter back of the team. This should consist of talks and questions on plays and generalship. Above all others, these men should know the rules correctly and perfectly.

Written questions and answers may be taken up early in the season, but later the work should be oral, as the men must learn to know the rules and just what commands to give instantly in the games.

The character of the questions should be such as will meet the needs of the men who are being developed. This can easily be done by watching the men in their work both in practice and in games. No two football players are exactly alike. Much less can two complete elevens be found with identical team characteristics. The captain and quarter back must study the individuality of every man on the team and must know just what he can do. A yard is a long distance when it stretches between the ball and the

opponents' goal on the third down, and it requires generalship to direct the play so that those three feet of space can
be negotiated. To know when and how to make the best
possible use of the material at hand is to solve a big
problem.

FRIDAY

It is well to spend Friday evening in singing and amuse-
ments and thus keep up the spirits of the men by varying
the monotony of the regular weekly routine. The coach
should aim to make the evening as pleasant as he can. It
is the night before the game. The minds of the men
should be taken off the contest that is due for the morrow.
Young players are anxious enough without the continual
reminders of which they have been the recipients all the
week, and the "Night Before" should be devoted to a good
rest.

The spirits of the men have probably been brought to
a high and intense pitch by the work of the week and they
should be allowed to enter the contest with fresh, rather
than fatigued minds.

SATURDAY

It is well on the evening after the game that the men
be given absolute freedom from any thought of the contest
just ended. They have probably earned a rest and should
be permitted to depart or remain as they choose. Monday
evening is time enough to talk over the game which took
place, and the men will then have had opportunity to ab-
sorb more thoroughly the situations which were presented
during the Saturday afternoon.

On the whole, these evening hours cement the team
man to man. The associations make them better acquainted.
They become chums and jolly fellows who can and will
play football of the best sort.

REQUIREMENTS OF THE INDIVIDUAL

The attainment of individual perfection is as impossible in football as in anything else, for absolute faultlessness does not exist in the human being. Nevertheless, a young fellow who is ambitious in athletics and who tries hard to outstrip others in the competition for football honors can greatly improve himself in the requirements of the individual. The fellow who has gone through the proper training honestly and courageously cannot but be a better man mentally and physically.

In the first place, a football player absolutely must be physically strong and rugged. The game gives no place for the weak and faint-hearted. It demands the stout and the brave. A large majority of young men are physically able to start. Out of the many who can with consistent training improve their bodies, only a few will do so. If you are with the majority in the first instance, start out with the motto, "I will," and you will succeed in the end.

STRENGTH AND BRAVERY A small man may be just as valuable a member of the team as the largest one on the eleven. Size is a good asset if the liabilities of other requirements do not offset it and leave a balance on the wrong side. Goliath was a big and mighty man but David was more than a match for him. There is hardly a "big team" which does not have some member who tips the scales somewhere around the 150-pound mark but who has won his place because he has made himself strong and courageous and is not afraid to perform the duties outlined for him.

SPEED Next to strength and bravery, the essential requirement is speed. A slow man has no place in the game. Quickness may be acquired just as strength may be developed. It is the jump on the other fellow that counts, and any player of a team who does not start his part with the rest of the formation at the proper instant may easily upset the entire play and spoil what otherwise would have been a good gain. Many people wonder why a team runs up and down the field, going through formations for hours during practice, with no opponents to stop them. It is to perfect speed as well as to acquire a knowledge of the signals and formations. A fast working team will always defeat a slow-running eleven.

ENDURANCE A football player must be a man not easily exhausted or injured. A game is not a severe strain on a man who is physically fit, because proper training has put him into such condition that he can speedily regain the loss caused by the tax on his strength. Taking out time for exhaustion or injury is giving the other side just as much rest and may be just what the opponents need. Other things being equal, the team with the endurance will wear down the opponents, and many a championship has been decided in the last few minutes of the game.

SAND This term, originally slang, but which has now become a word of general adoption, includes courage, grit and determination. These elements are absolutely essential to the successful player. Bravery, daring, firmness, resolution and unwavering decision "to do" are the factors which go to make the football player. The one who weakens or hesitates about tackling the opposing player running with the ball, even if that runner should happen to be the hardest man in the world to stop, will never make a football player. Football is not tag, and, no matter if the tackler does put his hand on the runner, the latter is not going to quit if he is a real football player. The runner must have the determination to get away and keep on advancing the ball and the tackler must have the firm resolution that his opponent must not be allowed to go a step further.

JUDGMENT AND VERSATILITY If you are ambitious to succeed in football do not be a machine player, but sum up every new situation and adapt yourself to it. Do not play your individual position the same way all the time. Vary your style and go at your man differently in each scrimmage. Out of the thousands and thousands of games that have been played there are never two exactly alike. Football affords more complications than chess and does not give the player nearly so much time to ponder. Judgment must be quick and accurate and the man who has a faculty of instantly adapting himself to a situation which suddenly presents itself is the man who makes a valuable member of the team. Conditions constantly arise in a football game which a player has never met before. In such a situation he has no time to go home and figure it out like a mathematical problem; he must act instantly, as would a colonel of a regiment suddenly surprised by an enemy. The ability to get out of a bad predicament or to keep the opponent from escaping, by a piece of strategy, when he gets into straits, is one of the essentials of a football player.

DISCIPLINE After all, a football team is but a small army and the discipline must be just as rigid as if something even more important than the mere winning or losing of a game were at stake. Orders must be obeyed unquestioningly after the team is on the field. The soldier who refuses to follow the mandates of his commanding officer is court-martialed, and the quicker the team gets rid of a member who willfully refuses to obey instructions, the better it is for the team. Rules for training, practice and play must be strictly adhered to if the team is to be a successful one.

SACRIFICE In a certain sense a player must lose his individuality and make himself a component member of his team. With the proper spirit of sacrifice in all its members, the team becomes harmonious. No man sinks more of his individuality than another, and any man who is to become a football player must be willing to sacrifice as much as any of his comrades. A young man may think that he is being deprived of so-called pleasures when he submits to the training rules necessary to make him a football player, but, as has been fully explained elsewhere, nothing is taken away from him that would do him any good. In football training he is simply following out directions which the best physicians in the land would advise as the proper method of living. Hence it ought not to be considered a sacrifice. Anything a man absolutely needs should be given him. The subtraction of necessities would be a sacrifice. The elimination of luxuries and pleasures is one that helps to build men up, not tear them down.

CONTROL OF TEMPER This would seem an almost unnecessary sub-head under this general chapter. It cannot but be admitted that the man who loses his head in a game is the man who will probably lose the game at a critical moment. It often occurs that an opponent makes use of a proficiency in sly banter for the very purpose of getting the other fellow "going." While tactics of this sort are not ideal in football, they are often presented in the general problem that the player meets. People on the sidelines do not appreciate the continual struggle going on in the individual player to control himself. To conquer an inclination to "get even" is a manly victory. If the resolution to accomplish this is fulfilled in the first game, it comes easier in the next contest, until it finally becomes second nature not to get "rattled." Nothing is better preparation for a young man to meet the plays on life's real gridiron without "losing his head."

SPIRIT No man ever made a success of anything unless his heart was in it. The wall street magnate loves his game on the stock exchange. The merchant king is inspired with a devotion to business. The great politician would go insane if it were not for his world of excitement and the opportunity which his field affords to give vent to his hobby. No lawyer or doctor ever approached the top of the ladder in his profession who did not have an enthusiasm in himself, constantly urging him higher. Likewise, no man can be a football player who does not love the game. Half-heartedness or lack of earnestness will eliminate any man from a football team. The love of the game must be genuine. It is not devotion to a fad that makes men play football; it is because they enjoy their struggle.

A prominent factor of success is the loyalty that the player must feel to his university or college. It is the inspiration that makes him do his utmost for the success of the team. His own individuality should be entirely sunken in what will redound most to the good of his Alma Mater. It is the spirit of loyalty and enthusiasm for the general cause that has made the American soldiers successful on so many battle-fields, and to this sentiment is due the successive victories of the Japanese over the Russians. The fire of loyalty is the greatest influence to animate a man in football as well as in any other form of competition.

GENERAL KNOWL- Lastly, the aspirant must master all the
EDGE OF THE GAME fundamentals of the game. The man
who cannot start, catch, pass, tackle, block and interfere
is not a real football player. There is no telling at what
moment he may be called upon to use his versatility to
save or to win the game. A championship contest may easily depend on whether one individual can catch a punt,
tackle a runner, block an opposing player or interfere
properly for his own team mate.

The requirements of the individual may seem numerous,
but they are important, and the man who comes nearest
to these ideals is the one who is going to make the greatest
player.

Illustrating how to plunge through the line.

SIGNALS

Signals in football enable a field captain to transmit his orders to his team in terms unintelligible to the opponents. The signalled commands are given in three ways: By signs, letters and numbers. At present, however, the number signals are most generally employed.

Whatever the system, it must primarily be plain and simple. It is, of course, absolutely necessary that the opposing team be unable to interpret the code employed. Still, this is a difficulty easily surmounted, for, when a team is executing plays with proper rapidity, the opponents do not have much time to think about signals other than their own which may be in use to assist them in stopping the attack. However, since the interpretation of signals is always possible to occur, and since the offensive team is very much weakened by the belief that its signals are known or likely to become known, an arrangement can easily be agreed upon for a change of the whole code, through the use of a new key number. Simple systems, too, allow such changes to be more easily made than do complicated ones.

The most important result of a system of simple signals is the rapidity with which it enables a team to play the game. The simplicity of the code should always be such that every member of the team can quickly grasp the meaning. Complicated signals necessarily make a team slow. Not only does a quarter find it difficult to accurately and quickly call the plays, but the men themselves will also have trouble in carrying out the complex commands. To secure quickness and smoothness of play it is imperative, even with the plainest signals, that each man on the team shall thoroughly know and understand each command and be able to respond as readily as he would to his own name and with just as little thought.

The men must be constantly drilled until the signals become a part of their very being. They must be so familiar with the entire code that there is no conscious mental action in connecting the signal with the play it calls for and the part they are to take in it. When the command is given each man should be ready instantly to start doing his work. Practically no time should elapse between the calling of the command and the comprehension by every member of the eleven of the play indicated. Not until the time that a team can grasp the plays instantly will it be able to play with machine-like quickness and precision and reach a stage of effectiveness otherwise impossible.

Since the quarter must start every play, it is best that it originate in his own mind and be signalled to the rest of the team by him and by no one else. Both theory and experience teach that a team can play faster if the quarter runs the game than if some other member is in charge.

Signals should never be drawled out slowly. They should be given in a clear-cut, snappy tone of voice. A team will always be much affected by the way in which a quarter calls his signals. One who is slow in this respect will have a slow-moving team behind him, while one who calls out his commands with a vigorous, decisive ring will find these same qualities imaged in the performance of his men in the succeeding plays.

The quarter should, as a rule, call a signal but once. Such a practice will find every man of the team alert to catch it as soon as it is given. When the signals are habitually repeated the team will soon become careless about catching the command the first time it is given, relying on the repetition, which accordingly becomes a very pernicious practice as, of necessity, the offense must wait until the signal is reiterated.

Sequence plays are a series of formations coming in a pre-arranged order and called for by one signal, which tells the players what series is to be used. They should not be used repeatedly in a game, because it is impossible to tell what results any one play may produce, while the sequence is likely to include plays with which the team finds it impossible to make headway against the opponents. Sequences can often be used to advantage, however, especially at the start of a game, for the purpose of speeding up the attack and sweeping the opponents off their feet before they realize what is happening. Again, a series is sometimes valuable when the cheering is at its highest, with the play near the sideline and the commands of the quarter back more difficult for his men to hear.

In arranging sequence plays attention should always be given to the possession of a series which can be used in each distinct part of the field, one near the sideline, one in the center of the field and one near the goal line of the opponents. Only plays that are good and sure ground-gainers should be employed in the sequence, and no series should include over four or five plays.

The following is an easy and practical set of signals: Let each play be numbered, one number only being needed to give the men their cue. Number the first play "five," the next "six," and so on. For example, let "five" and "six" represent the play that will send the respective half backs straight into the line from their regular positions. All even numbers will call for plays that go to the left of center. while all odd numbers call for attack on the right. The reverse, of course, is just as effective. Then continue to number the plays as follows: "Seven," full back buck on the right of center; "eight," full back to the left of center, and so on, to include all the varieties of attack that the team may learn all through the season.

The following illustrates how the plan may be used:

"Three"—Left half cross-bucks outside right tackle.

"Four"—Right half cross-bucks outside left tackle.

"Five"—Right half straight ahead.

"Six"—Left half straight ahead.

"Seven"—Full back bucks center on the right.

"Eight"—Full back bucks center on the left.

"Nine"—Left tackle around through right tackle from regular position.

"Ten"—Right tackle around through left tackle from regular position.

"Eleven"—Left half back cross-bucks outside of right tackle with left tackle back.

"Twelve"—Right half cross-bucks outside of left tackle with right tackle back.

The tackle-back formation on the right can be called "formation A;" tackle-back on the left can be called "formation B," and so on for each of the other formations desired.

Formation signals, calling for changes from the regular positions, should be called before the men line up for the play after the preceding down. This saves much time, and there is no excuse for the quarter's permitting the men to take their regular places only to change from one position into another before the play can be started.

The numbers 20, 30, 40, 50, 60, 70, 80, 90, and other multiples of ten should never be actual signal numbers, as their use will interfere with the intelligibility of the signals, from the ambiguity which might arise in the game.

The calling of the working signal may be guarded in different ways. For instance, it may be the second number called in the series by the quarter back. In such a case, "11-(7)-9-8" would call for play No. 7, which is the full back through on right of center. Again, "7-(3)-18-4" would send the left half back cross-bucking outside of right tackle. Both of these plays are shown in the accompanying diagram.

If the quarter comes to suspect his signs have been noted by the opponents, he can readily change the real signal number to the third or even the first number which he calls out. With this added precaution it becomes practically impossible for an enemy to maintain a knowledge of the signals to an extent which will assist in pre-determining the direction of the plays.

Another code of signals, the basic principle of which is in common use, is as follows:

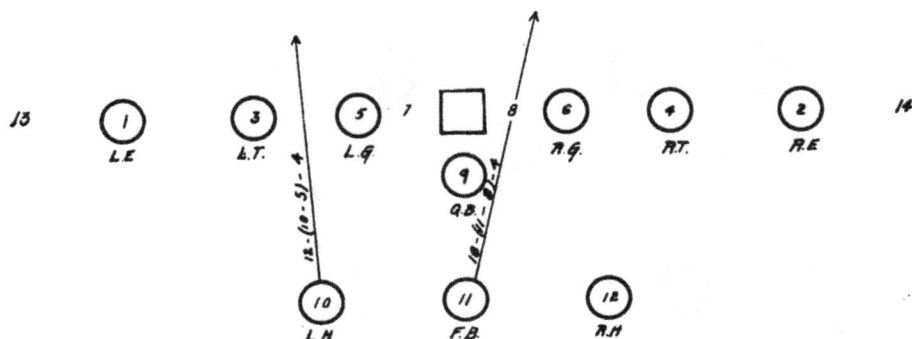

It will be noticed in this diagram that the men are all numbered, those on the left side of the line being odd while those on the right are even numbers. There are also numbers 13, 14, 7 and 8, which do not represent men but are necessary to show the point of attack. The point of attack will sometimes be the number of the player occupying the position indicated, but in this instance will represent the hole or position just outside the player.

Suppose that the left half back is to carry the ball between left guard and left tackle, the signal given will be "12-(10-5)-4. (See diagram.) The second number given is 10, the number of the left half back. The third number, 5, it that of the left guard and the play is therefore an attack outside of the man playing the position of the third number given.

In the same way the signal "18-(12-13)-6" directs the right half back to carry the ball around position 13, which is outside of the opposing end. The signal "6-(3-4)-8" accordingly means that the left tackle is to carry the ball around from his position through tackle. Similarly, "12-(11-7)-6" indicates that the full back is to buck the center on the left side, while "18-(11-8)-4" would call for a center buck on the right side.

It is necessary to use in connection with such a system of signals a series of formation commands. "Formation A" would thus represent a tackle-back play as seen in the following diagram:

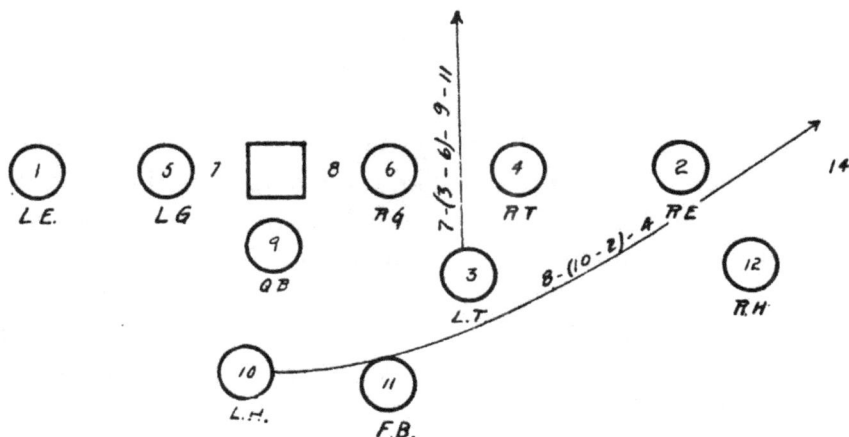

From this formation the signal "8-(10-2)-4" might be given, which would send the left half back with the ball just outside the right end position, while "7-(3-6)-9-11" would mean that the left tackle is to carry the ball straight ahead between right guard and right tackle.

From these illustrations it can easily be seen how any number of plays and formations can be worked out from this system.

TEAM PLAY

The evolution of football from the crude form in which the game began to the present stage of perfection it has attained rests almost entirely on the development of team play. Where originally one man, relying almost entirely on his own efforts, bore the brunt of his own particular play, whether offensive or defensive, now the efforts of ten others are also exerted to the same end for which he is working.

The players of the old school, mighty men though they were, and equal, beyond a doubt, in individual ability to the men who are playing the game today, would be helpless when confronted with the systematized attack and defense of an eleven with anything like their natural ability, coached in the finer points of the game which have been evolved by the football students of modern times.

To the perfection of team play, which has become necessary in a successful eleven of the present day, is due, no doubt, the tremendous strides which the game has made in popularity. The spectator who appreciates the finer points of the game glories in an eleven which works together, and the members of the team themselves are welded into closer harmony by the feeling of mutual obligation which the team play brings with it. The confidence that is felt by the man chosen to bear the brunt of the play, when he knows that his comrades will be there to help him, each in his assigned place, contributes to the efforts of an eleven the ideal feeling of team spirit and makes each game increasingly attractive to those who participate in the play on the field.

Showing fine interference—team play.

To strengthen the impression in the mind of each of his ten comrades that he himself may be relied on to do his part should form the foremost endeavor of every member of the team. He must show the others that, when the emergency comes, as it does come in every play, he is doing his duty. With such zeal firmly instilled in the mind of each man, football reaches its highest state of perfection.

The center and guards must enter upon their task in each game with a unified purpose. To take care of one's immediate opponent should not be the sole aim of each man. He should, in addition, be able and anxious to extend to his comrades the aid which they may need. Should one of the opposing trio stand out above the others as a dangerous man, two men should combine their efforts that he may be taken care of, instead of shifting the entire responsibility on his immediate team mate. The same relations should exist between the tackles and the ends. The backs must return, to their utmost ability, the protection which they are receiving from their line, by a combined aggressiveness on attack and a support on defense that will make the members of the line confident that their efforts are not in vain.

Each man must be on the alert to discover instantly any hint regarding the enemy's tactics which may be of benefit to his own side. The eyes of the captain cannot be everywhere at once and often a shift in the position of one of the opponents, a tendency to precede a play by a glance, a false start or some other indication, unseen by the rest, may give a premonition which, if immediately communicated by signal, may prove of inestimable value.

On offense, team play has developed along the lines of interference and helping the runner. As soon as a play is called each man should be ready to fulfill one certain pur-

pose. If in the line, he must block his man long enough
to make sure that the opponent cannot break through and
spoil the play before it has gotten fairly started. Then he
must place himself, if possible, ahead of the play, where
he will be in a position to help the runner, either by warding off tacklers or assisting him to shake off men who may
be in the act of bringing him down.

If a back or a member of the attacking column, the
player should not confine his efforts to warding off from
the runner the man whom he is there to care for. He
should do this, of course, and after it is done, should endeavor to rejoin the runner in his course down the field,
there to take care of further attack, thus making an even
longer gain possible.

If the runner, he should be calculating with lightning
speed the openings which are being made for him by his
interference. When he has passed in safety the first line
of defense he must study how best to avail himself of the
interference that remains, slowing down, if necessary, to
allow one of his comrades to fall into place, or charging
intrepidly at the least thoroughly guarded point, should his
efforts be unassisted and there be no prospect of reinforcements.

There is no feature of football more beautiful than a
long run in circumstances like these. The rush of the attacking phalanx against the rampart of bone and brawn;
the melting away of the interference as it disposes of the
men in the path of the runner; the emerging of the man
with the ball into the open field and the judgment which he
exercises, combined with his own strength and speed, call
for the very highest ability.

In an instant the good player will take an inventory of
the situation. Far out from the line of scrimmage, running

to his aid, he perceives one of his comrades. In front of him, charging with outstretched arms, is a hostile tackler. A dodge, and the foe misses his clutch by an inch. The ·time is short but the interferer is now close up. Ahead is another member of the opposing team. The runner, his plan formed, slows down, circles a bit, and has acquired a comrade to help him. Combined they charge the approaching enemy. While the interferer blocks his man the runner circles once more. It may now be a clear field to a touchdown that he sees before him. Only his own speed is necessary in this case to keep him ahead of the pursuing members of the opposing team. It is team play that has made it possible.

How many times it occurs that, when the line has been successfully assaulted and a runner penetrates into the enemy's territory, one of his comrades who has also broken through is able to grasp the man with the ball and carry him out of the arms of the tacklers into the enemy's country still further! It is team play.

While the development of modern team play is more plainly evident in attack than defense, the latter department of the game has also been greatly improved by the discovery of methods through which combinations can be made to offset the efforts of a systematic attack. Especially when a play is hinted at in advance, as is invariably the case when a kick is to be made, combination of forces at one point may result in a counter attack which will nullify the plan. Some member of the line may be pushed through by his comrades right into the path of a play, or the point at which an attack is directed may be suddenly strengthened in order to meet it successfully. It is team play again.

Even in the kicking department, which still remains the

closest approach to individual effort retained by the game in its advanced stage, team play is always prominent. Of what use is a competent kicker unless he receives an accurate pass from his center? His best efforts may be unavailing, for he may never be able to get the ball away. Even when successfully kicked, the ball may be brought back by the opponents to a distance which may nullify the value of the effort, unless the other members of the kicker's team are able to tell in advance the direction in which the ball is to be sent, the distance and height designed for its flight and the other data necessary to guide them swiftly down the field to recover its possession, if possible, and, if not, to tackle the man who has caught the ball, before he is able to bring it back any appreciable distance. Once more, this is team work.

Eleven men make up a football team now, as in the early days of the game, but modern requirements make it necessary that these eleven men play constantly to one end. If one of them lags, errs or is inefficient, it is almost impossible for the others to get results, no matter how well directed may be their efforts. Individual strength, wit, courage and agility must be there, but they must weld themselves into a chain that makes every advantage possessed by one of the members of the eleven a common asset —one that is used to its utmost and on every possible opportunity. For the last time, it is team play and only team play that will yield success, and no eleven can get along without it.

PHOTOGRAPHS OF FORMATIONS AND DIAGRAMS OF PLAYS

The following pictures and diagrams are used to illustrate just how to execute the various plays given. The pictures show the formations and the exact positions each individual should assume. By consulting this the player can tell just where to line up in his proper place; the men are lettered so each player can tell just where he should be. The diagrams following each illustration show how to execute the different plays from that same formation. The positions of the men in the diagrams are lettered just like the men lined up in the formation. The plays given are for one side of the line only—they can all be worked on the opposite side just as well. The diagrams show just where each man should go in each play, and the reading under the diagram tells him just what he should do. An explanation of the diagram is as follows:

The square always represents the center.
The other men are represented by circles.
The solid black circle is the player to carry the ball.
A solid double line shows the course the runner should go.
A single solid line is the direction of the men in the interference who are ahead of the runner.
A single dotted line is the path that should be followed by the men who are to help the runner from the side or from behind.
A double dotted line represents the ball as passed by a toss.
A single solid line from one player to another means that the ball is passed by being handed.

Regular formation showing the position for every man to assume.

Photo by Lyndon.

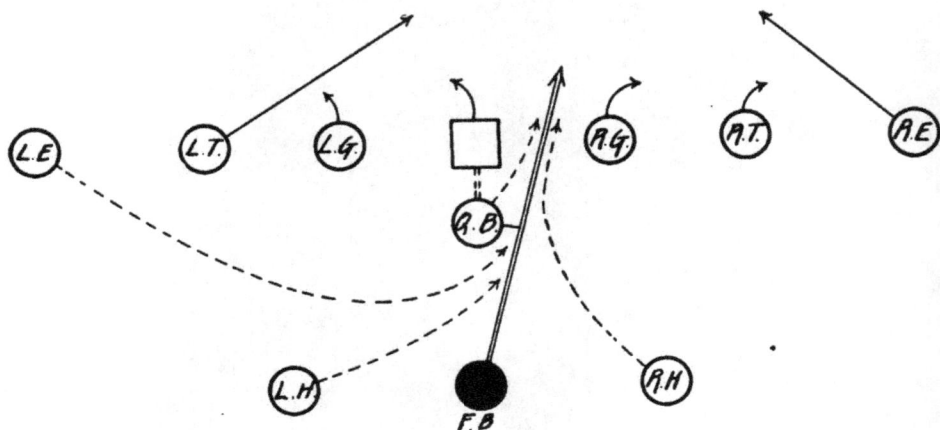

Regular Formation—Full Back Plunge Through Center.

This is the quick mass play on right of center.

Center blocks opposing center to left.

Left Guard helps throw opposing center to left.

Right Guard blocks opposing guard out to right.

Left Tackle breaks through and cuts off opposing half back and assists runner.

Right Tackle assists in throwing opposing left guard out.

Left End comes around quickly and pushes from behind.

Right End blocks opposing tackle out and goes through and assists the runner.

Quarter Back passes ball to full back, then helps hold him up and carry him forward.

Left Half Back assists runner on the left hip.

Right Half Back assists runner on right hip.

Full Back takes ball and goes in low and hard to keep feet as long as possible.

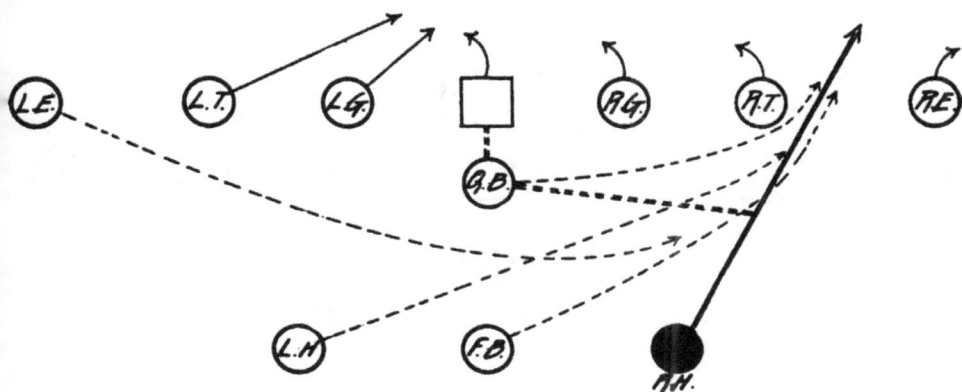

Regular Formation—Right Half Back Straight Ahead Through Right Tackle.

This is a quick opening play and should strike almost at the position occupied by offensive right tackle.

Center blocks his man to the left.

Left Guard assists in throwing opposing center to the left.

Right Guard blocks opposing left guard to the left.

Left Tackle breaks through behind opposing line, cuts off full back and assists runner.

Right Tackle assists in blocking opposing left guard to the left.

Left End comes around and assists runner from behind.

Right End blocks opposing tackle out.

Quarter Back helps hold the runner up and carries him forward.

Left Half Back assists the runner on the left hip.

Right Half Back receives the ball from the quarter by a toss and plunges low into the line.

Full Back assists the runner on right hip.

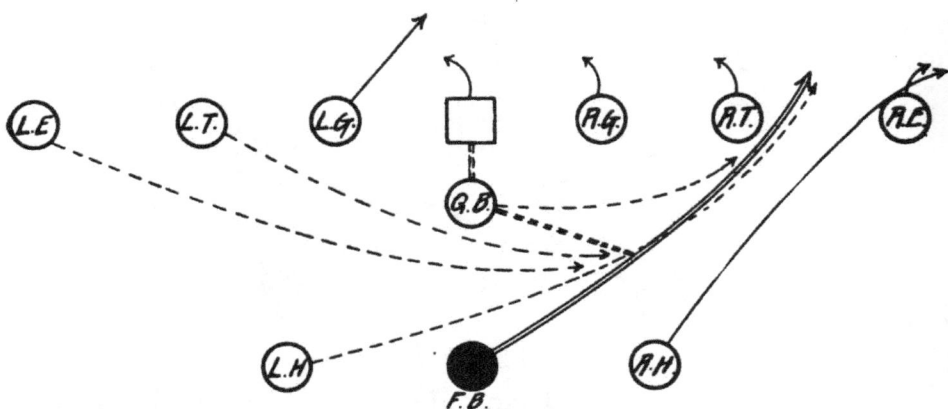

Regular Formation—Full Back Mass on Right Tackle.

This play is in the nature of a revolving mass on tackle.

Center blocks opponent to left.

Left Guard goes through, cuts off reinforcements and assists the runner.

Right Guard blocks opponent to left.

Left Tackle comes around quickly and assists the full back on the left hip.

Right Tackle assists in blocking opposing guard to left.

Left End follows around and pushes from the rear.

Right End blocks opposing tackle out.

Quarter Back helps carry the runner from the inside.

Left Half Back assists the runner on the right hip.

Right Half Back goes ahead of the runner and assists the right end in blocking the right tackle out.

Full Back carries the ball.

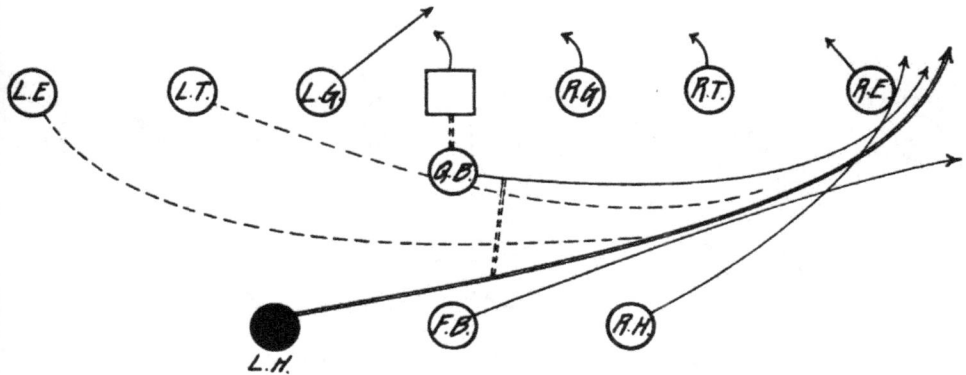

**Regular Formation—Left Half Back Cross Buck Outside
of Right Tackle.**

This is in the nature of a quick driving play directly
over the position occupied by the defensive right end.

Center blocks opponent to left.

Left Guard goes through, cuts off reinforcements and assists the runner.

Right Guard blocks the opponent to left.

Left Tackle comes around and assists the runner by his
interference.

Right Tackle blocks opposing guard and assists in check-
ing opposing tackle.

Left End comes around quickly, watching for a fumble and
carries runner forward when tackled.

Right End boxes opposing tackle.

Quarter Back passes ball to left half on the run, keeping
ahead of him for interference.

Left Half Back is the runner.

Right Half Back goes forward quickly and blocks opposing
back in toward tackle.

Full Back blocks opposing end out.

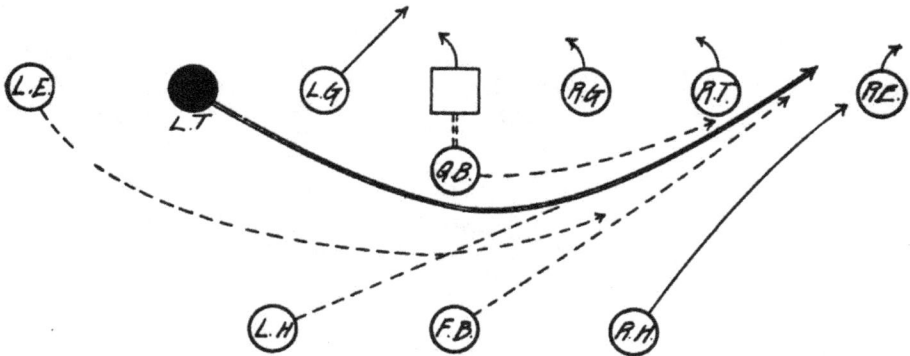

Regular Formation—Left Tackle Around Through Right Tackle.

This play should not be attempted on a wet field.

Center blocks opponent to left.

Left Guard goes through, cuts off reinforcements.

Right Guard blocks opponent to left.

Left Tackle leaves position quickly, swings close around quarter, who hands him the ball, and strikes the opening between tackle and his own right end.

Right Tackle blocks opposing guard in.

Left End follows and assists the tackle from the rear.

Right End blocks opposing tackle out.

Quarter Back assists the runner on the left side, keeping him on his feet and carrying him forward.

Left Half Back pushes from behind.

Right Half Back goes ahead of the runner and assists right end in blocking opposing tackle.

Full Back assists the runner on right hip.

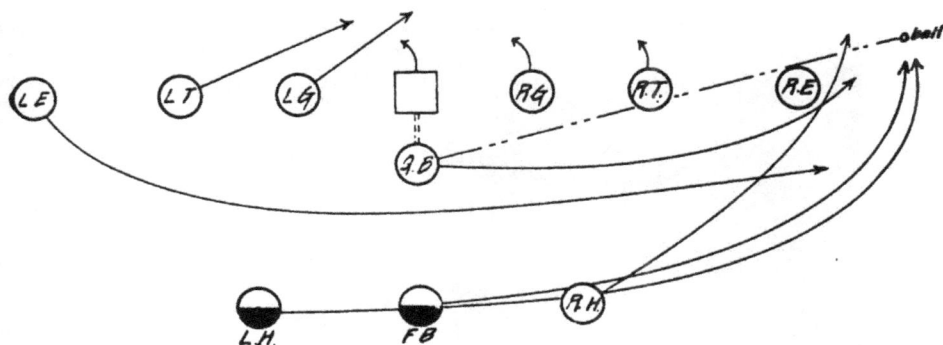

Regular Formation—Quarter Back Kick.

This play should not be used when the ball is likely to be kicked out of bounds or when opposing ends are playing very wide.

Center blocks opponent to left.

Left Guard goes through immediately and blocks any of the opposing backs possible.

Right Guard blocks opponent to left.

Left Tackle goes through and cuts off reinforcements.

Right Tackle protects kicker and blocks to the left.

Left End comes around rapidly to secure ball if blocked or to tackle runner if opponent secures the ball.

Right End blocks opposing tackle or half back.

Quarter Back, after kicking ball, should secure it if possible or assist any of his own men who do.

Left Half Back and Full Back should stay on side until kick is made and the one in the best position should secure it, the other one interfering.

Right Half Back should go directly forward and block any opponent who attempts to get the ball.

Tackle-back—the same formation can be used on left side. Right half must be outside right end. *Photo by Lyndon.*

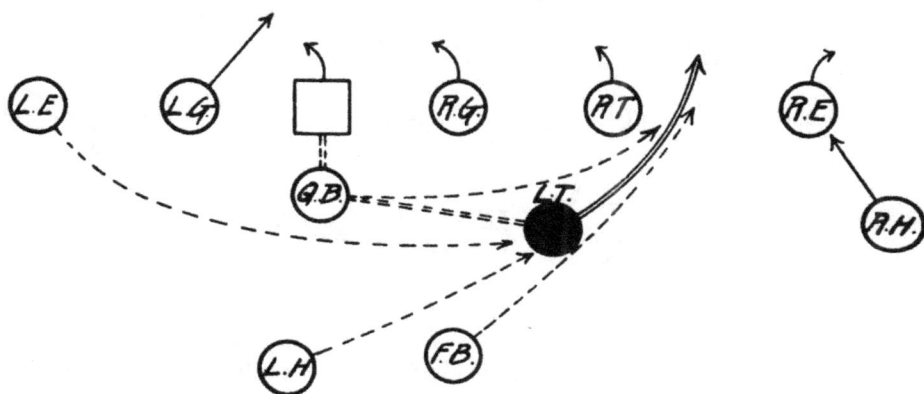

Tackle Back Formation—Tackle Straight Ahead.

This is a quick, line-driving play.

Center blocks opponent to left.

Left Guard breaks through and cuts off reinforcements.

Right Guard blocks opponent to left.

Left Tackle carries the ball, going low and hard.

Right Tackle blocks opposing guard in.

Left End comes around and assists the runner on left hip.

Right End blocks opposing tackle out.

Quarter Back assists the tackle by carrying him forward
    and holding him up.

Left Half Back pushes from the rear.

Right Half Back assists in blocking opposing tackle out.

Full Back assists the runner on the right hip.

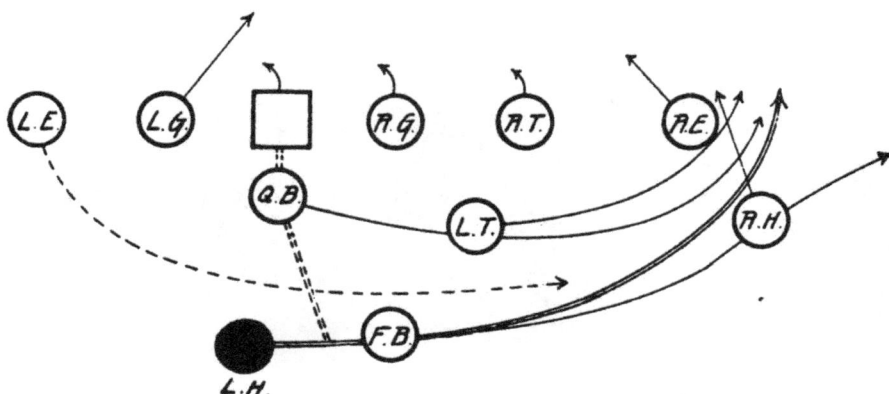

**Tackle Back Formation—Left Half Back Cross-Bucks
Outside Right End.**

This play should be a quick running play.

Center blocks opponent to left.

Left Guard goes through, cuts off reinforcements and joins
the runner.

Right Guard blocks opponent to left.

Left Tackle follows right half in the interference, blocking
to the left.

Right Tackle blocks opposing guard in.

Left End follows runner and assists him in any way
possible.

Right End boxes opposing tackle.

Quarter Back passes ball to the runner on the run and follows left tackle in the interference.

Left Half Back is the runner.

Right Half Back assists in blocking opposing tackle, if
necessary; if not, takes opposing half.

Full Back blocks opposing end out.

Tackle Back Formation—Full Back Mass on Tackle.

This is in the nature of a revolving mass play.
Center blocks the opponent to the left.
Left Guard goes through and assists the runner.
Right Guard blocks to the left.
Left Tackle blocks opposing end out.
Right Tackle blocks opposing guard to left.
Left End follows and assists from behind.
Right End blocks opposing tackle.
Quarter Back assists in carrying the runner forward.
Left Half Back assists the runner on the right hip.
Right Half Back blocks opposing tackle or half back, which-
   ever is needed.
Full Back carries the ball.

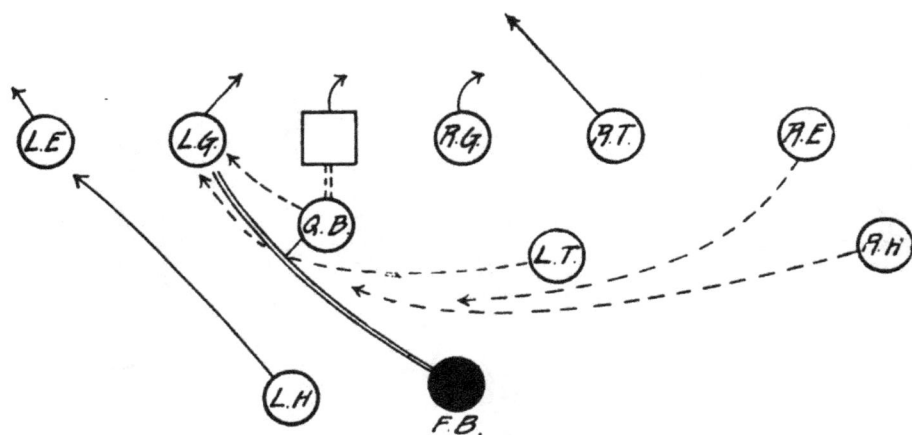

Tackle Back Formation—Full Back Buck Over Left Guard.

This play to be used if opposing linemen are shifting to the right.

Center blocks to the right.

Left Guard blocks opposing guard to the right.

Right Guard blocks opposing guard out.

Left Tackle assists runner on left hip.

Right Tackle breaks through, cuts off reinforcements, and and assists the runner.

Left End blocks opposing tackle out.

Right End follows around and pushes the runner.

Quarter Back assists the runner by holding him up and carrying him forward.

Left Half Back assists left end in blocking opposing tackle out.

Right Half Back pushes in the rear.

Full Back carries the ball over the left guard position.

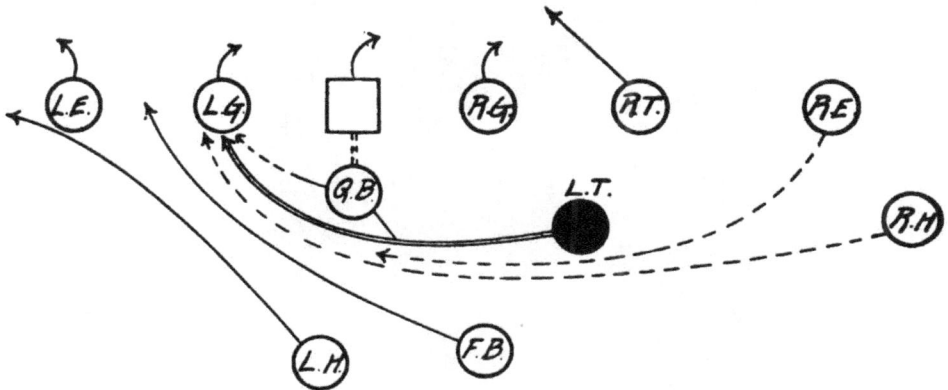

Tackle Back Formation—Tackle Cross-Buck.

This play is effective especially when opponents are shifting to meet this formation.

Center blocks opponent to the right.

Left Guard blocks opponent to the right.

Right Guard blocks opponent to the right.

Left Tackle carries the ball over position occupied by left guard.

Right Tackle breaks through, cuts off the reinforcements and assists the runner.

Left End blocks opposing tackle out.

Right End follows runner and assists from the rear.

Quarter Back assists the runner by holding him up and helping him forward.

Left Half Back assists left end in blocking opposing tackle out.

Right Half Back assists the runner on left hip.

Full Back goes through opening ahead of runner clearing the way.

Tackle-back play in action, illustrating how the men should charge in the line and run in the interference. *Photo by Lyndon.*

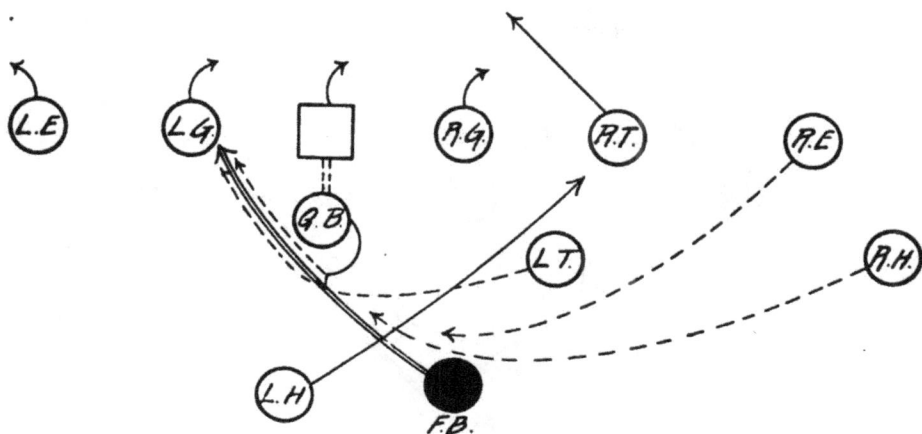

Tackle Back Formation—Fake Attack—Full Back Buck on Left Side.

This is a fake interference play, left half going across as if to attack the right side.

Center blocks opponent to the right.

Left Guard blocks opponent to the right.

Right Guard blocks opponent to the right.

Left Tackle assists the runner on the left hip.

Right Tackle breaks through, blocks off reinforcements.

Left End blocks opposing tackle out.

Right End comes around and assists the runner from behind.

Quarter Back turns as if to pass the ball to the left half back and then turns on around and passes to full back for a plunge through left guard. He should assist the runner by carrying him forward.

Left Half Back runs off right tackle with all appearances of having the ball.

Right Half Back comes around and pushes from the rear.

Full Back carries the ball. He should hesitate an instant before starting.

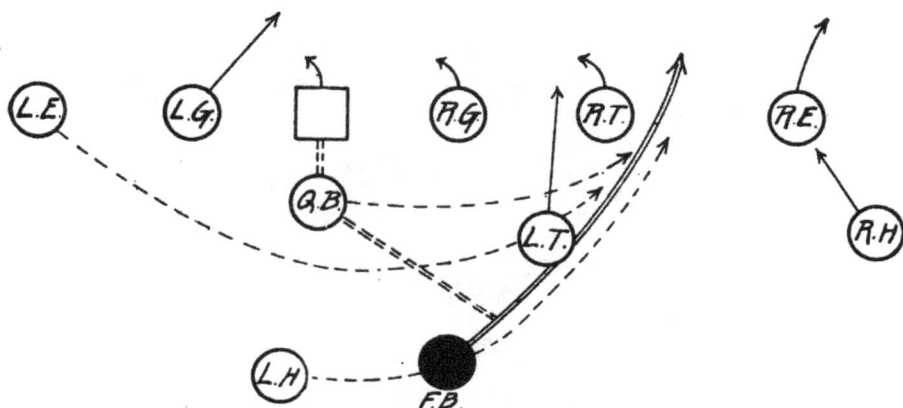

Tackle Back Formation—Full Back Plunge Through Right Tackle.

This play should not follow in the direction the left tackle charges, but should appear to do so at the start and then swerve off to the right.

Center blocks opponent to the left.

Left Guard goes through, cuts off opposing half back and assists the runner.

Right Guard blocks to the left.

Left Tackle charges forward low between right guard and right tackle, blocking opposing guard.

Right Tackle blocks opposing defensive back.

Left End runs around and assists from the rear.

Right End blocks opposing tackle out.

Quarter Back assists the runner by holding him up.

Left Half Back assists the runner on the right hip.

Right Half Back assists in blocking opposing tackle out.

Full Back takes the ball.

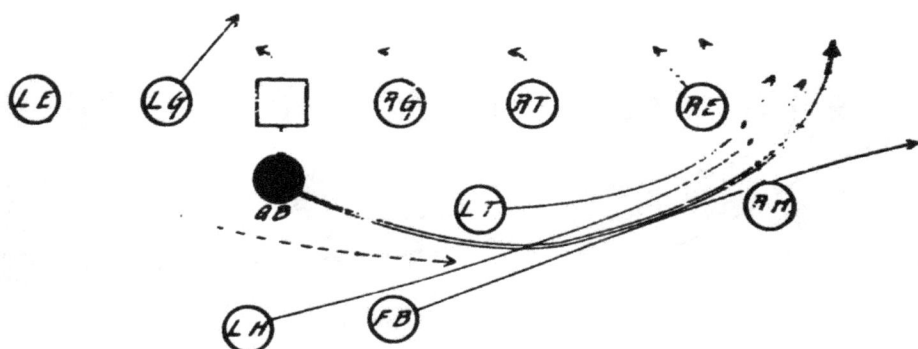

Tackle Back Formation—Quarter Back Run.

This play should be attempted if opposing ends are playing in close and the quarter back is good at carrying the ball.

Center blocks opponent to the left.

Left Guard goes through, blocks opposing back and joins the runner if possible.

Right Guard blocks opponent to left.

Left Tackle follows the right half in the interference and blocks the first man he meets.

Right Tackle blocks opposing guard in.

Left End follows the runner and renders him any assistance possible.

Right End blocks opposing tackle.

Quarter Back is the runner with the ball.

Left Half Back follows left tackle in the interference.

Right Half Back blocks opposing tackle if necessary; if not, takes opposing half.

Full Backs blocks opposing end out or in, whichever is best.

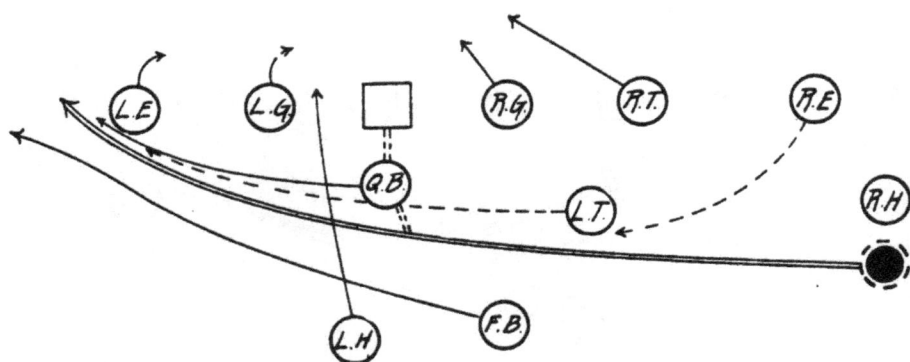

Tackle Back Formation—Right Half Back Run Around Left End.

This play should be made very quickly. The right half back must be speedy and get away quickly.

Center blocks opponent to the right.

Left Guard blocks opponent to the right.

Right Guard goes through.

Left Tackle protects runner from inside.

Right Tackle goes through and cuts off opponents' half back.

Left End boxes opposing tackle.

Right End comes around and assists from behind.

Quarter Back passes ball to half back and goes ahead for interference.

Left Half Back plunges forward into line as if the attack were at center.

Right Half Back is the runner.

Full Back blocks opposing end.

Tackle Over on Line Formation—the backs are shifted slightly to right.   *Photo by Lyndon.*

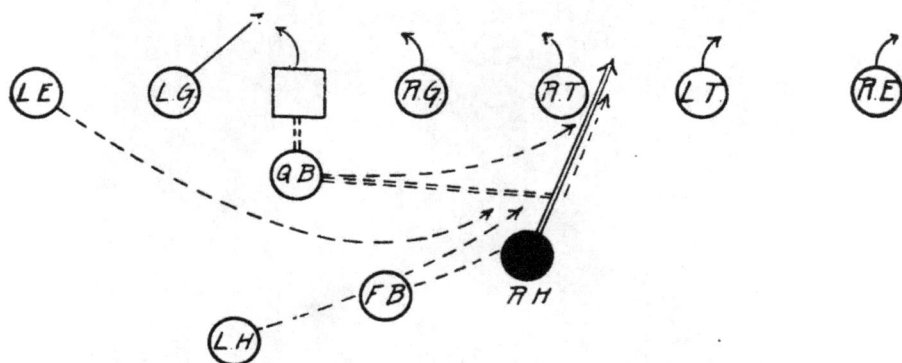

Tackle Over Formation—Right Half Back Straight Ahead.

This play should be able to make ground between two strong tackles.

Center blocks opponent to left.

Left Guard breaks through and blocks off any of opponents' back-field men.

Right Guard blocks opponent to left.

Left Tackle blocks opposing tackle out.

Right Tackle blocks opposing guard to left.

Left End follows around and joins in the push.

Right End assists in blocking tackle out.

Quarter Back helps carry half forward.

Left Half Back assists runner on left hip.

Right Half Back takes ball and goes in low and hard.

Full Back assists runner on outside hip.

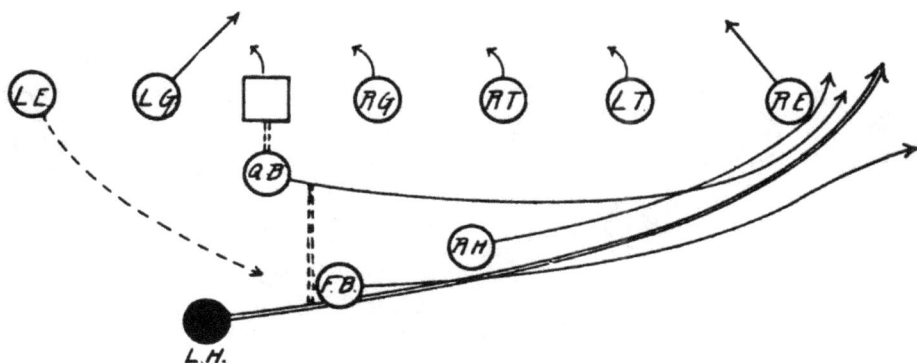

Tackle Over Formation—Left Half Back Run Around Right End.

This play must get away quickly and go fast.

Center blocks to left.

Left Guard breaks through and blocks off half back—joins runner if possible.

Right Guard blocks to left.

Left Tackle blocks to left.

Right Tackle blocks to left.

Left End follows and assists in any way possible.

Right End boxes opposing tackle.

Quarter Back passes ball to left half on the run and goes ahead in the interference.

Left Half Back is the runner.

Right Half Back blocks opposing back.

Full Back blocks opposing end.

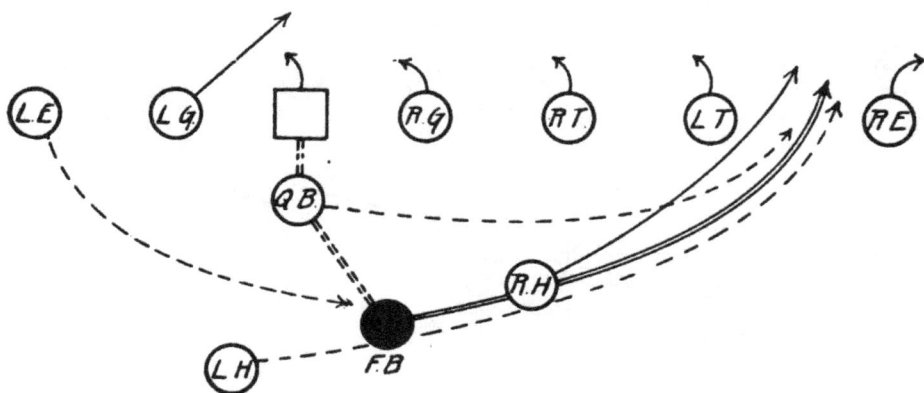

Tackle Over Formation—Full Back Mass on Tackle.

This is a quick-moving mass play. All must get in and help.

Center blocks to left.

Left Guard breaks through and cuts off reinforcements.

Right Guard blocks to left.

Left Tackle blocks to left.

Right Tackle blocks to left.

Left End comes around and pushes from behind.

Right End blocks tackle out.

Quarter Back helps runner along from the left side.

Left Half Back assists runner on right hip.

Right Half Back goes ahead and clears the way.

Full Back is the man with the ball.

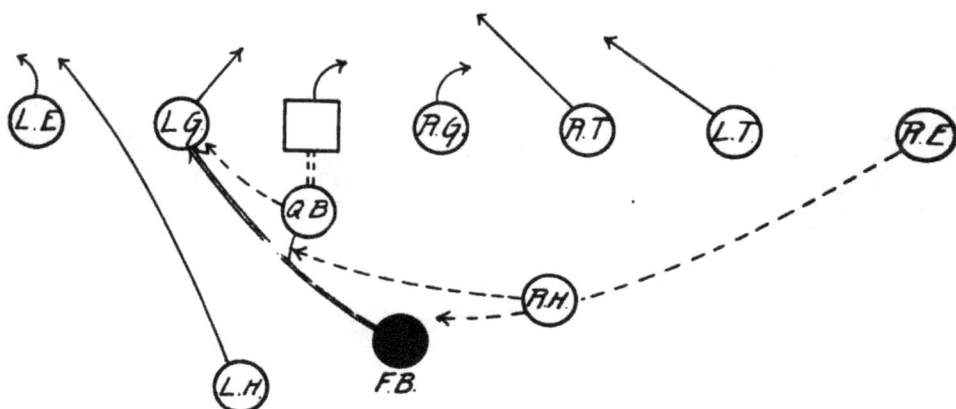

Tackle Over Formation—Full Back Cross-Buck Over Left Guard.

This play should be executed quickly when started.
Center blocks to right.
Left Guard blocks to right.
Right Guard blocks to right.
Left Tackle goes through.
Right Tackle goes through and assists runner.
Left End blocks opposing tackle out.
Right End follows around fast.
Quarter Back carries full back forward.
Left Half Back assists left end to block tackle out.
Right Half Back pushes full back from behind.
Full Back carries the ball over left guard position.

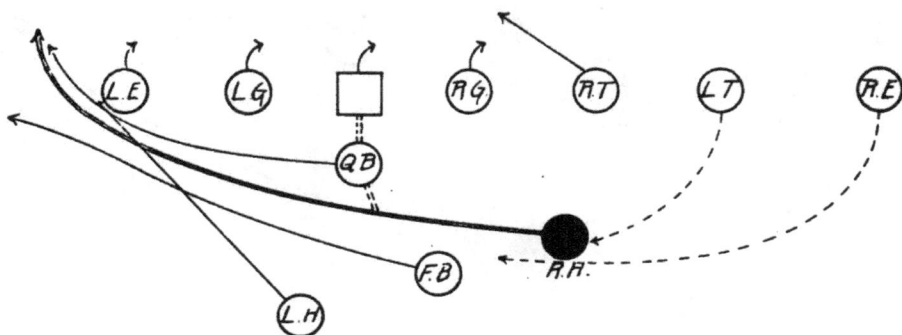

Tackle Over Formation—Right Half Back Cross-Buck.

Play to be used if opponents are shifting.
Center blocks to right.
Left Guard blocks to right.
Right Guard blocks to right.
Left Tackle follows and protects runner from inside.
Right Tackle breaks through and cuts off reinforcements.
Left End boxes opposing tackle.
Right End follows and assists runner.
Left Half Back blocks opposing half.
Right Half Back is the man with the ball.
Full Back takes opposing end.

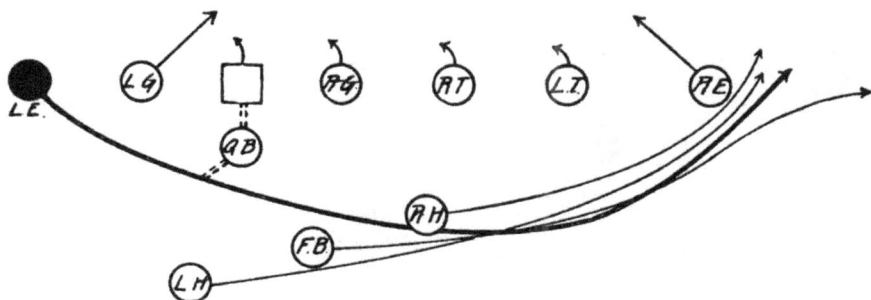

Tackle Over Formation—Left End Around.

Play should not be used on a slippery field.

Center blocks to left.

Left Guard breaks through and joins runner.

Right Guard blocks to left.

Left Tackle blocks to left.

Right Tackle blocks to left.

Left End gets away quickly and takes the ball by a toss from the quarter back.

Right End blocks opposing tackle.

Quarter Back passes ball and goes ahead and interferes for runner.

Left Half Back follows right half in interference.

Right Half Back blocks opposing half back.

Full Back blocks opposing end.

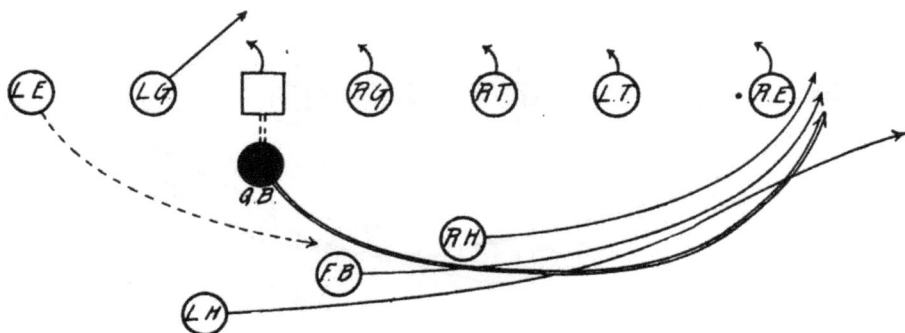

Tackle Over Formation—Quarter Back Run.

A good play to use if the opponents are playing close on defense. It will open them up or the play will make ground.

Center blocks to left.

Left Guard breaks through and cuts off reinforcements.

Right Guard blocks to left.

Left Tackle blocks to left.

Right Tackle blocks to left.

Left End follows and aids in any way he can.

Right End blocks opposing tackle.

Quarter Back is the runner.

Left Half Back blocks opposing end.

Right Half Back blocks opposing tackle or half.

Full Back follows right half back in the interference.

Tandem—Tackle Over Formation—Different men can be used in the tandem.   Photo by Lyndon.

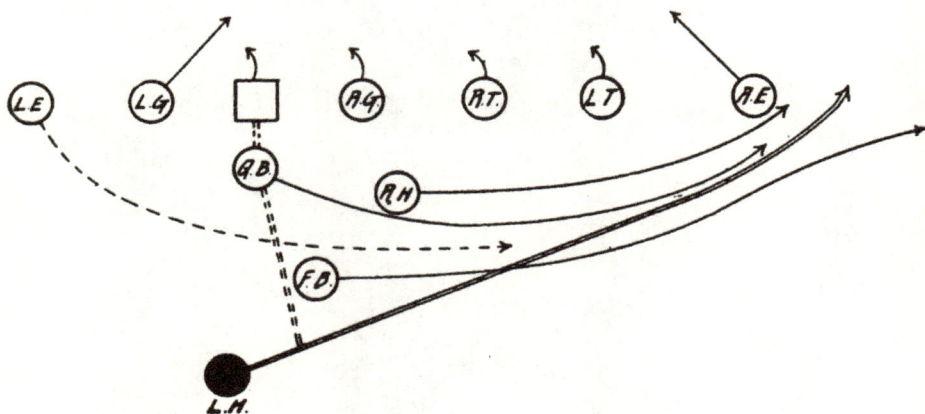

Tandem—Tackle Over—Left Half Back Cross-Buck.

This play must be executed rapidly.

Center blocks to left.

Left Guard breaks through, blocks half back.

Right Guard blocks to left.

Left Tackle blocks to left.

Right Tackle blocks to left.

Left End follows and assists.

Right End boxes opposing tackle.

Quarter Back passes ball quickly and gets into the interference.

Left Half Back is the runner.

Right Half Back blocks opposing half back.

Full Back blocks opposing end.

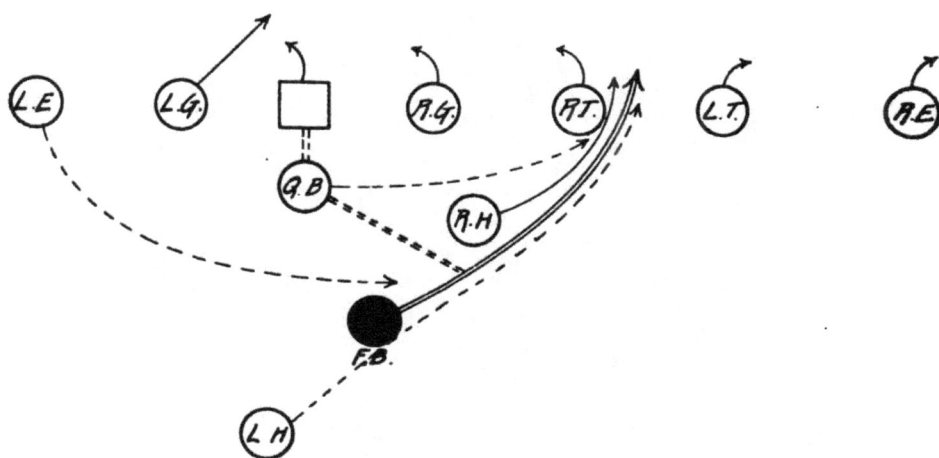

Tandem—Tackle Over—Full Back Buck.

This play should be executed with a dive, instead of a slow mass play.

Center blocks to left.

Right Guard breaks through and blocks opposing backs to left.

Left Guard blocks to left.

Left Tackle blocks to right.

Right Tackle blocks to left.

Left End follows around and pushes.

Right End blocks opposing tackle out.

Quarter Back helps the runner.

Left Half Back assists the runner on right hip.

Right Half Back goes ahead of runner.

Full Back takes the ball.

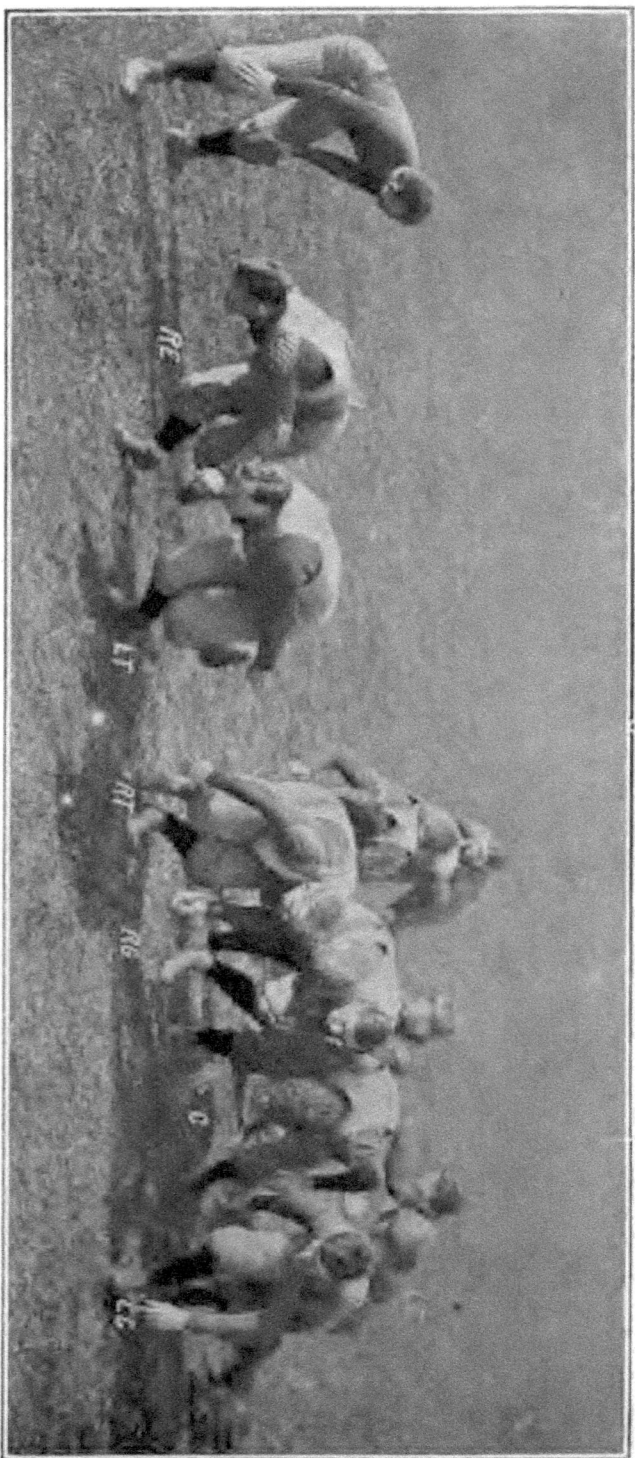

The Tandem in Action.—Illustrating how the men charge in the line and how the backs get away. *Photo by Lyndon.*

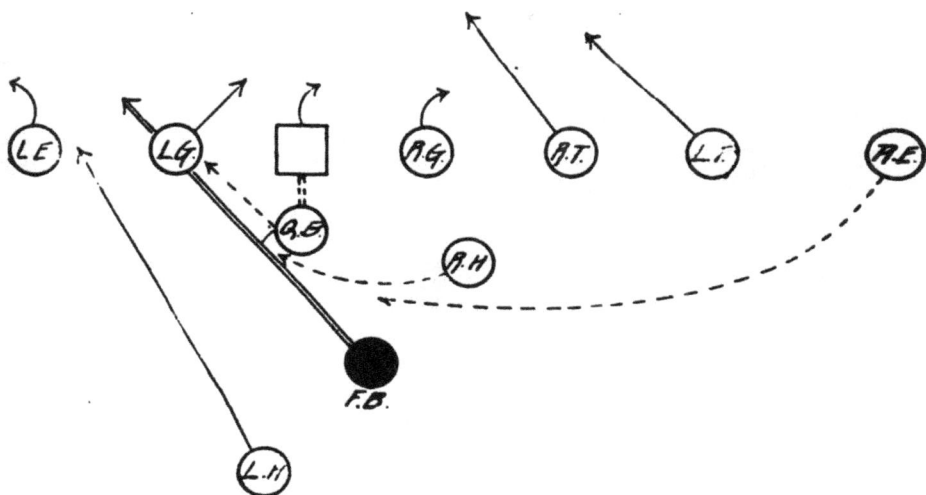

Tandem—Tackle Over—Full Back Buck.

Can be used if opponents shift.
Center blocks to right.
Left Guard blocks to right.
Right Guard blocks to right.
Left Tackle breaks through.
Right Tackle breaks through, blocks off backs.
Left End blocks tackle out.
Right End follows around.
Quarter Back helps the runner.
Left Half Back assists left end in blocking tackle out.
Right Half Back follows runner through.
Full Back takes the ball through left guard.

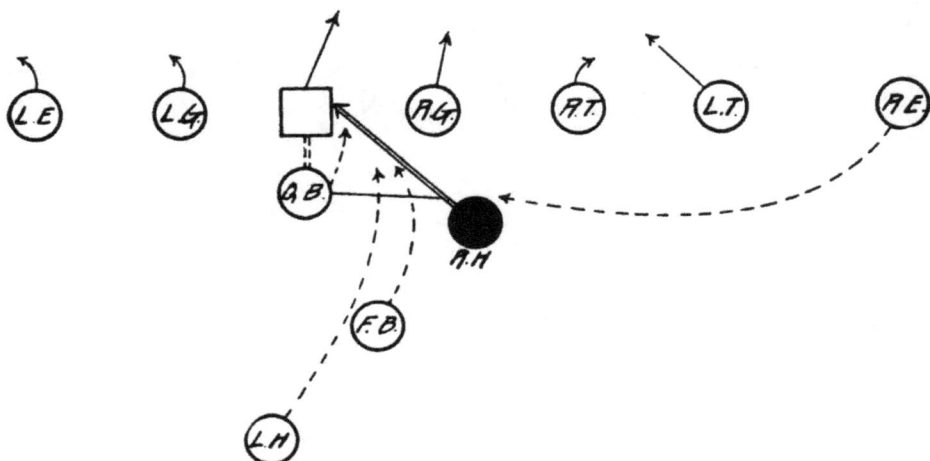

Tandem—Tackle Over—Right Half Back Cross-Bucks.

This is a close, driving, mass play on center.

Center charges ahead and to the right.

Left Guard blocks to left.

Right Guard blocks to right.

Left Tackle breaks through.

Right Tackle blocks to right.

Left End blocks opposing tackle out.

Right End follows.

Quarter Back carries runner forward.

Right Half Back is the runner.

Left Half Back and Full Back push from behind.

Showing position of men in the tandem and their relative position, also proper position for quick starting.
Photo by Lyndon.

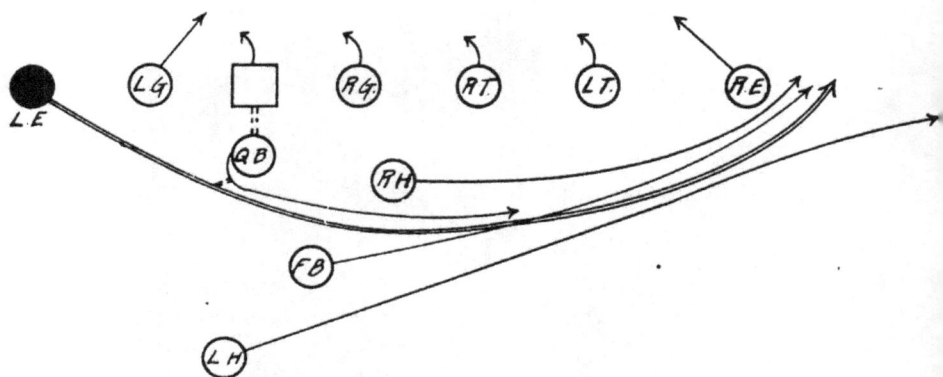

Tandem—Tackle Over—Left End Around.

Center blocks to left.
Left Guard blocks to left, goes through.
Right Guard blocks to left.
Left Tackle blocks to left.
Right Tackle blocks to left.
Left End comes around rapidly and takes the ball.
Right End boxes opposing tackle.
Quarter Back passes ball to end and then makes interference.
Left Half Back, Right Half Back and Full Back all go
    ahead for interference.

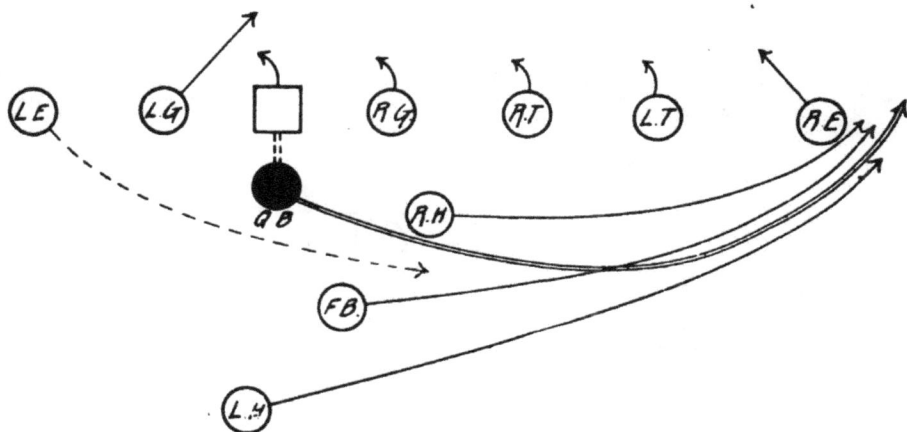

Tandem—Tackle Over—Quarter Back Run.

This play to be successful must be executed rapidly.
All the interference must "hurry up."
Center blocks to left.
Left Guard breaks through, joins runner.
Right Guard blocks to left.
Left Tackle blocks to left.
Right Tackle blocks to left.
Left End follows around.
Right End boxes tackle.
Quarter Back is the runner.
Left Half Back blocks opposing end.
Right Half Back blocks opposing half.
Full Back follows right half back in the interference.

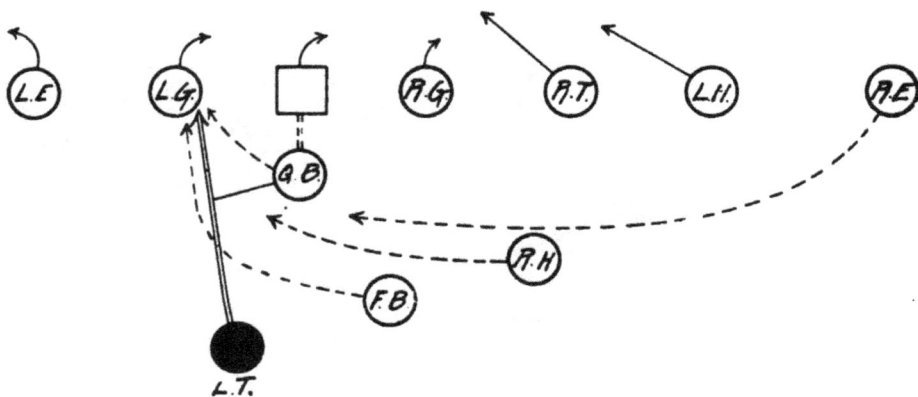

Tackle Straight Back—Left Tackle Straight Plunge.

In this play the tackle bucks straight ahead over the position occupied by left guard.

Center blocks to right.

Left Guard blocks to right.

Right Guard blocks to right.

Left Tackle is the man to take the ball.

Right Tackle blocks opposing backs to right and assists runner.

Left End blocks tackle out.

Right End comes around and pushes from behind.

Quarter Back carries the tackle forward.

Left Half Back breaks through and assists.

Right Half Back assists runner on right hip.

Full Back assists runner on left hip.

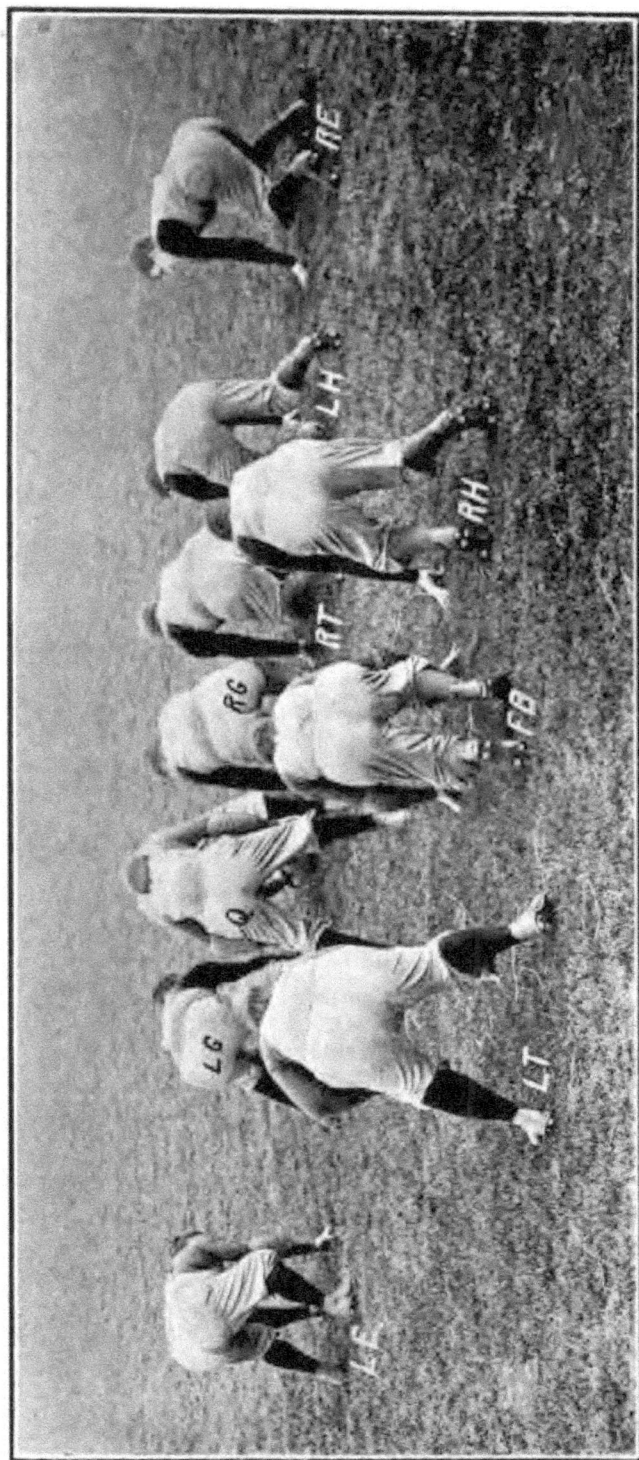

Photo by Lyndon.

Tackle back in half back position.

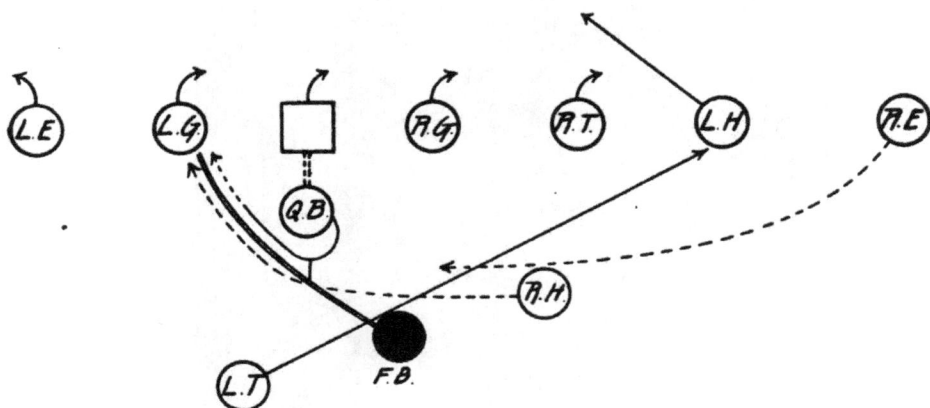

Tackle Straight Back—Full Back Cross-Buck.

This is a feint attack by left tackle on the right side of the line, and the full back makes the real attack at left guard position.

Center blocks to right.

Left Guard blocks to right.

Right Guard blocks to right.

Left Tackle starts as if to carry ball to right.

Right Tackle blocks to right.

Left End blocks opposing tackle out.

Right End follows and assists from behind.

Quarter Back turns as if to pass ball to left tackle and turns on around and passes ball to full back and then assists runner.

Left Half Back breaks through and assists.

Right Half Back assists runner on left hip.

Full Back is the runner.

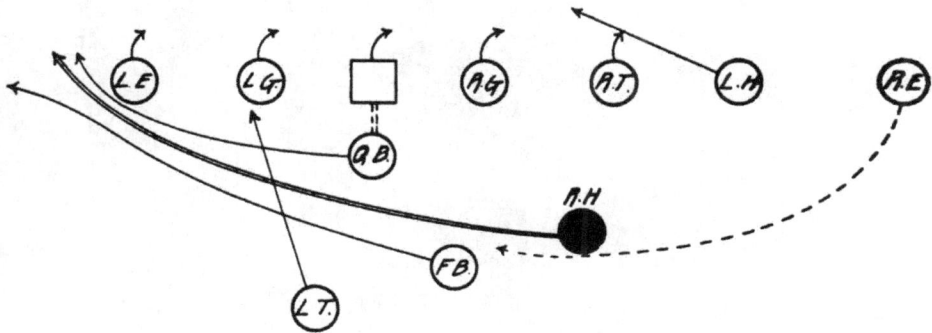

Tackle Straight Back—Right Half Back Cross-Buck.

This play is more in the nature of a run than a plunge and must be pulled off fast.

Center blocks to right.

Left Guard blocks to right.

Right Guard blocks to right.

Left Tackle goes straight into the line and appears to take the ball.

Right Tackle blocks to right.

Left End boxes tackle.

Right End follows and assists runner.

Quarter Back makes a bluff at passing ball to left tackle and then passes it to right half, then goes ahead in the interference.

Left Half Back breaks through and joins runner.

Right Half Back takes the ball.

Full Back blocks opposing end.

Tackle Back Square.—A very strong formation for close, quick, concentrated attack.

Photo by Lyndon.

Tackle Back Square—Left Tackle Plunge Through Center.

This is a close mass play. Execute slowly; all hold together.

Center charges his man straight back and to the right.

Left Guard blocks to the left.

Right Guard blocks to right.

Left Tackle takes the ball.

Right Tackle blocks opponent to right.

Left End goes through and assists runner.

Right End hurries around and joins in the push.

Quarter Back assists runner by holding him up and helping him forward.

Left Half Back assists on left hip.

Right Half Back blocks to the left.

Full Back assists on right hip.

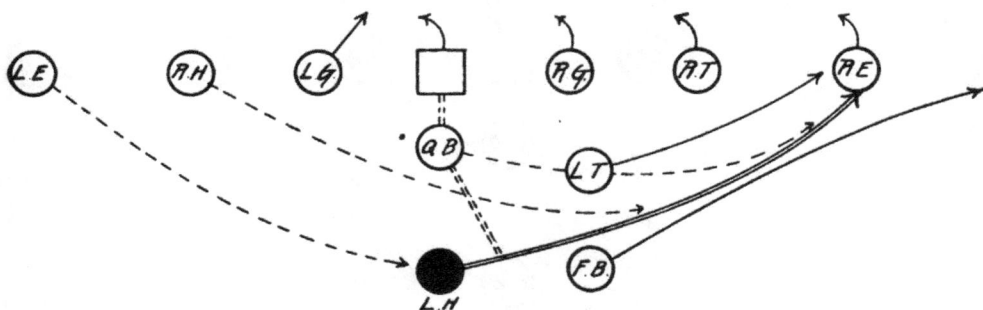

Tackle Back Square—Left Half Back Run Around Tackle.

This play should go off quickly.
Center blocks to left.
Left Guard goes through, joins runner.
Right Guard blocks to left.
Left Tackle leads interference.
Right Tackle blocks opponent to left.
Left End follows.
Right End boxes opposing tackle.
Quarter Back assists runner from inside.
Left Half Back takes the ball.
Right Half Back comes around for interference.
Full Back blocks opposing end.

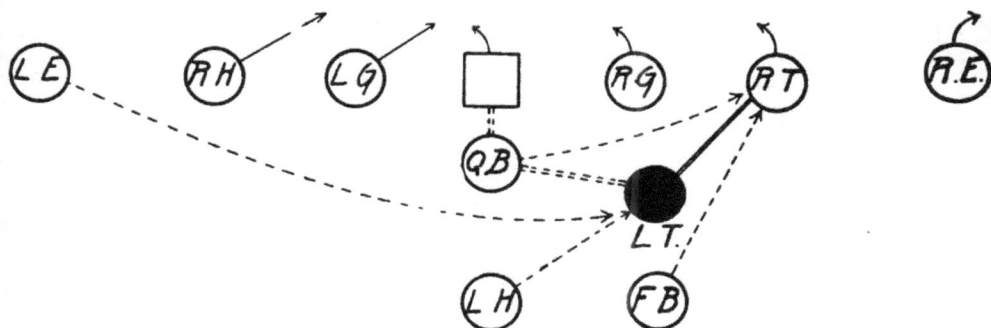

Tackle Back Square—Tackle Straight Plunge.

This is a slow mass play on or just inside opposing tackle.

Center blocks to left.

Left Guard goes through and blocks to left.

Right Guard blocks to left.

Left Tackle takes the ball.

Right Tackle blocks to left.

Left End follows around and joins in the push.

Right End blocks tackle out.

Quarter Back assists in helping runner ahead.

Left Half Back assists runner on left hip.

Right Half Back goes through.

Full Back assists runner on left hip.

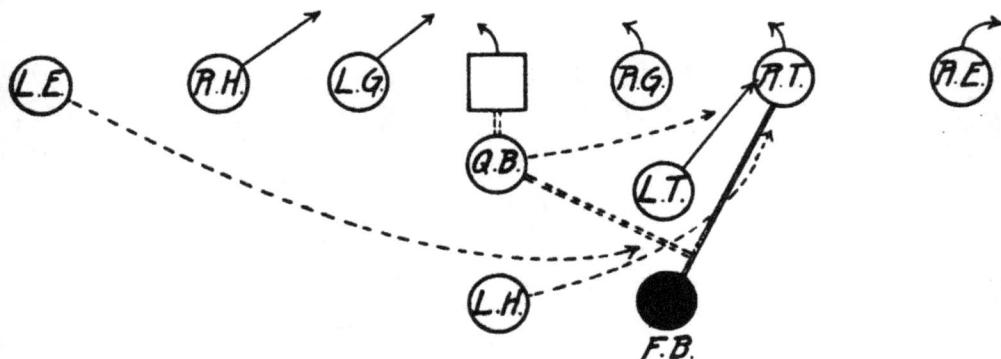

Tackle Back Square—Full Back Plunge.

The full back should follow the path of the left tackle.
Center blocks to left.
Left Guard goes through to assist.
Right Guard blocks to left.
Left Tackle leads the interference through the line.
Right Tackle blocks to left.
Left End comes around and joins in the push.
Right End blocks tackle out.
Quarter Back assists the runner to keep his feet and go
    ahead.
Left Half Back assists on right hip of runner.
Right Half Back goes through and across to assist.
Full Back carries the ball.

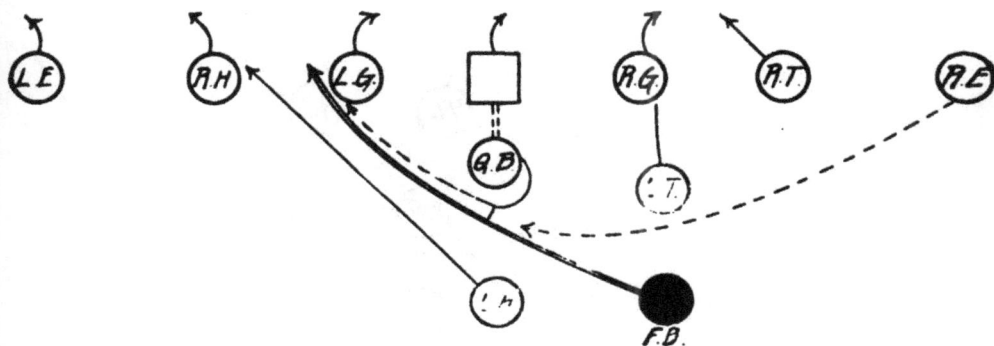

Tackle Back Square—Full Back Cross-Buck.

This is a feint to hit the right side of the line, but full back cross-bucks over left guard.

Center blocks to right.

Left Guard blocks to right.

Right Guard blocks to right.

Left Tackle goes ahead and appears to take ball for plunge through the guard-tackle hole.

Right Tackle goes through and assists.

Left End assists, blocking tackle out.

Right End comes around and pushes.

Left Half Back goes through ahead of runner.

Right Half Back blocks tackle out.

Full Back takes the ball.

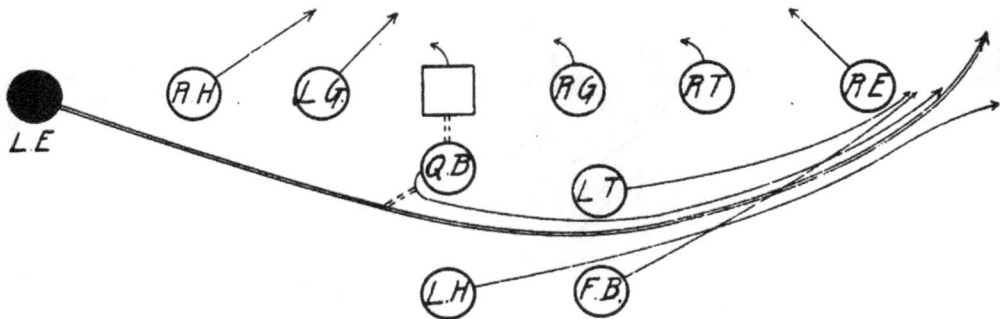

Tackle Back Square—Left End Around.

This play must get away rapidly and keep going. It should not be attempted on a wet field.

Center blocks to left.

Left Guard goes through.

Right Guard blocks to left.

Left Tackle leads the interference.

Right Tackle blocks to left.

Left End must hurry.

Right End boxes tackle.

Quarter Back passes ball and goes ahead in the interference.

Left Half Back blocks opposing end.

Right Half Back goes through and joins runner.

Full Back follows left tackle in the interference.

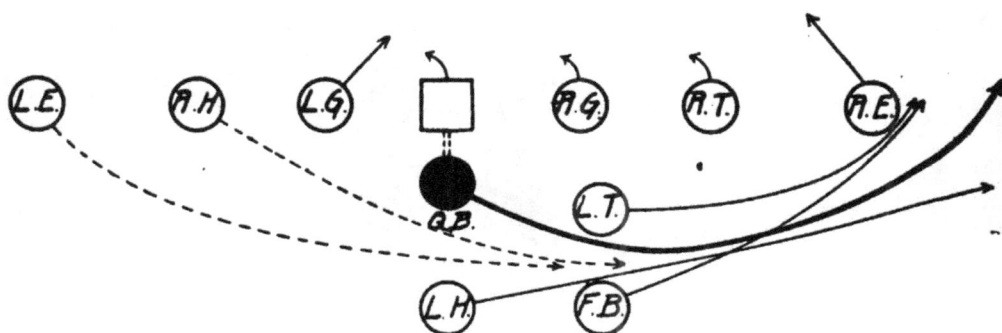

Tackle Back Square—Quarter Back Run.

Like all plays that strike wide from the center, this play must be executed rapidly.

Center blocks to left.

Left Guard goes through and joins runner.

Right Guard blocks to left.

Left Tackle heads the interference.

Right Tackle blocks to left.

Left End follows and protects runner.

Right End boxes opposing tackle.

Quarter Back must go fast.

Left Half Back blocks opposing end.

Right Half Back aids the runner by coming around for
    interference.

Full Back follows the left tackle in the interference.

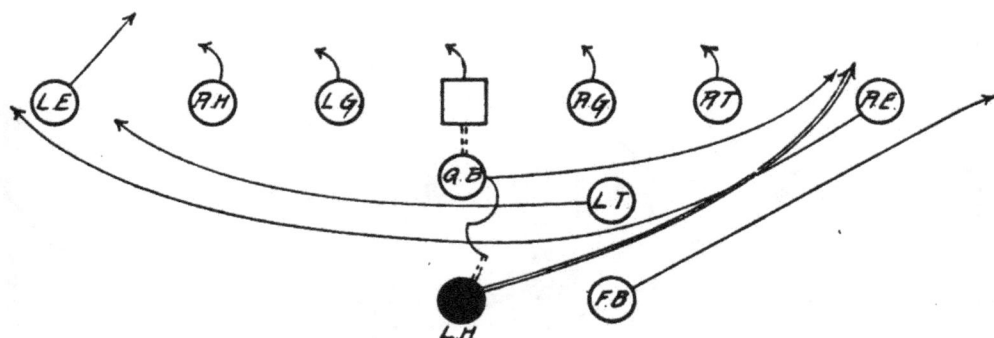

Tackle Back Square—Delayed Pass.

The success of this play will depend largely on the concealment of the ball by the quarter back and the way the right end carries out his part.

Center blocks to left.

Left Guard blocks to left.

Right Guard blocks to left.

Left Tackle leads the feint attack around the left.

Right Tackle blocks to left.

Left End goes through and blocks defensive full back.

Right End comes around and appears to take the ball from quarter back for run around left end.

Quarter Back makes a bluff at passing ball to right end, holds it concealed a moment and then passes to left half back.

Left Half Back waits for ball and then goes through right side.

Right Half Back blocks to left.

Full Back interferes for right half back.

Tackle Straight Back Formation.

Photo by Lynton.

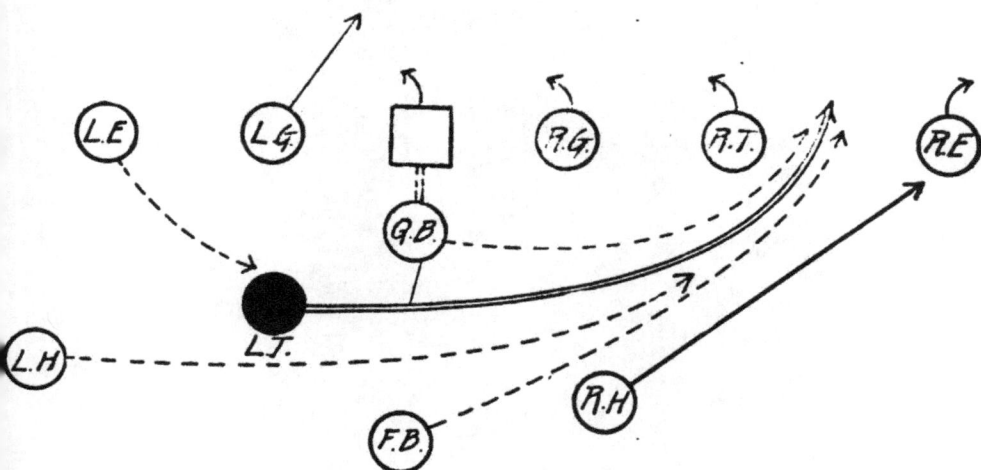

Tackle Straight Back Formation—Left Tackle Cross-Buck.

This play strikes on the strong side.   The men should take their positions in the formation as they line up; not go to the regular formation and then shift.   Should be played quickly after the men are in position.

Center blocks to the left.

Left Guard breaks through and assists runner.

Right Guard blocks to the left.

Left Tackle takes the ball.

Right Tackle blocks to the left.

Left End follows and assists from behind.

Right End blocks opposing tackle out.

Quarter Back carries the runner forward from the inside.

Left Half Back follows the runner and pushes from behind.

Right Half Back assists right end in blocking opposing tackle out.

Full Back assists runner on right hip.

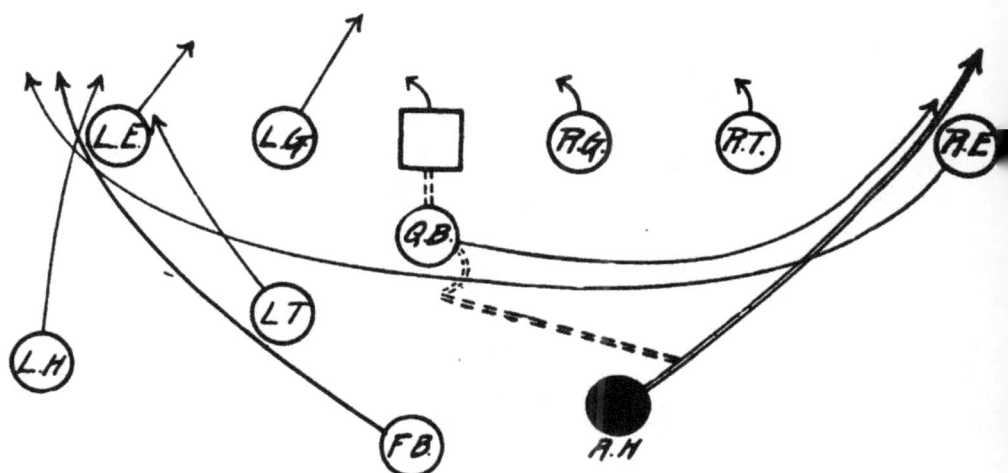

Tackle Straight Back Formation—Delayed Pass.

The success of this play will depend largely on the deception used by the right end and the quarter back.

Center blocks to the left.

Left Guard blocks to the left and breaks through.

Right Guard blocks to the left.

Left Tackle follows left half back in a feint on the left side.

Right Tackle blocks to the left.

Left End goes through to block opposing full back.

Right End comes around quickly and makes a bluff at taking the ball, and continues on as if he had it.

Quarter Back appears to pass the ball to right end, conceals it for a moment and then passes it to right half back, getting into the interference for the right half back if possible.

Left Half Back blocks opposing half back.

Right Half Back hesitates until quarter is ready to pass him the ball and then takes the ball and goes through the right side.

Full Back follows left half back and left tackle in the feint attack on left side.

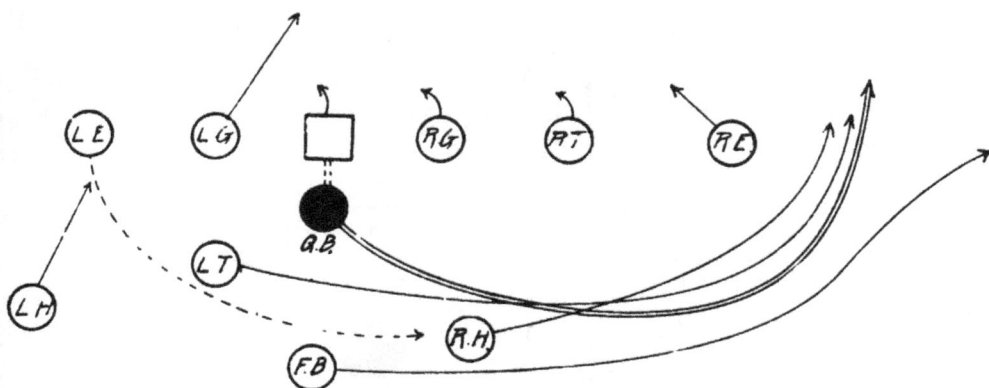

Tackle Straight Back Formation—Quarter Back Run.

This play should meet with success if the opponents are shifting to meet the tackle-back formations and the play is executed rapidly.

Center blocks to the left.

Left Guard goes through, blocks opposing half back and joins the runner.

Right Guard blocks to the left.

Left Tackle follows the right half back around in the interference.

Right Tackle blocks to the left.

Left End follows the runner.

Right End blocks opposing tackle.

Quarter Back is the runner on a direct pass.

Left Half Back blocks off anyone attempting to follow.

Right Half Back leads the interference and blocks defensive back.

Full Back blocks opposing end.

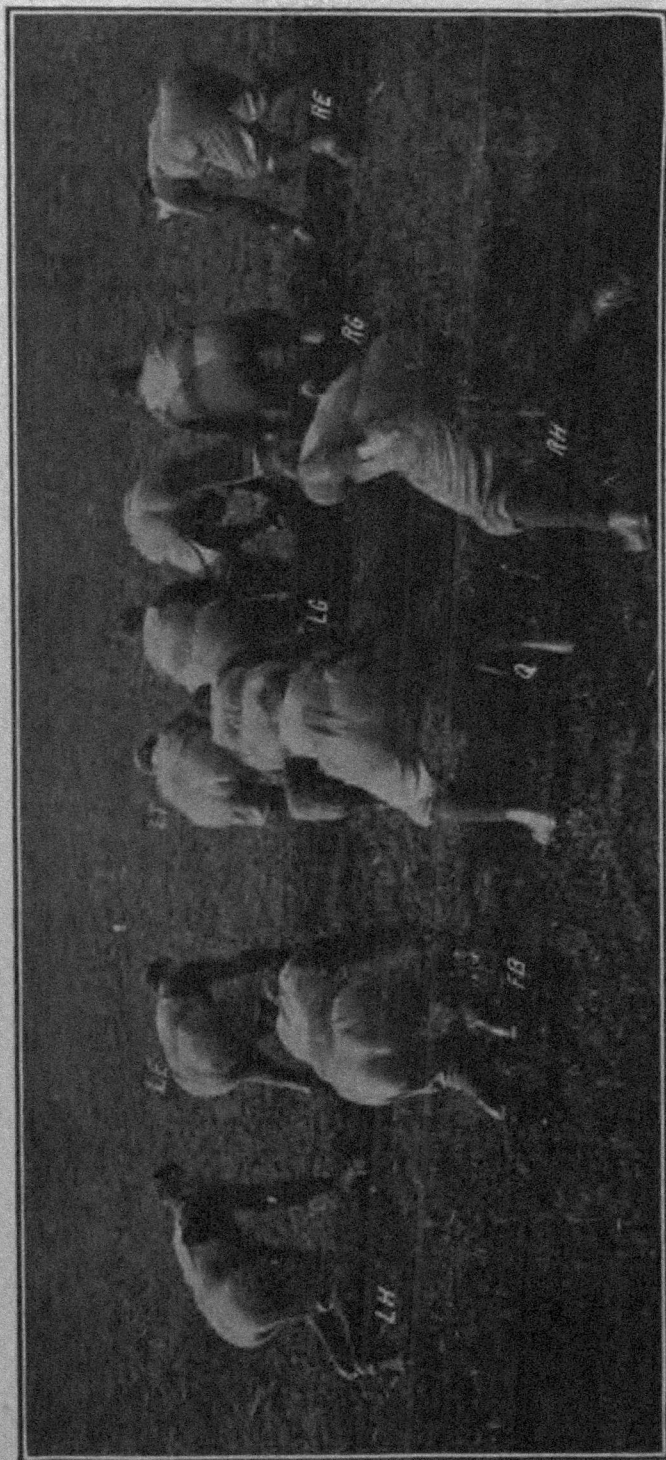

Direct Pass Formation.—Ball passed directly to half back or to any other runner.   *Photo by Lyndon.*

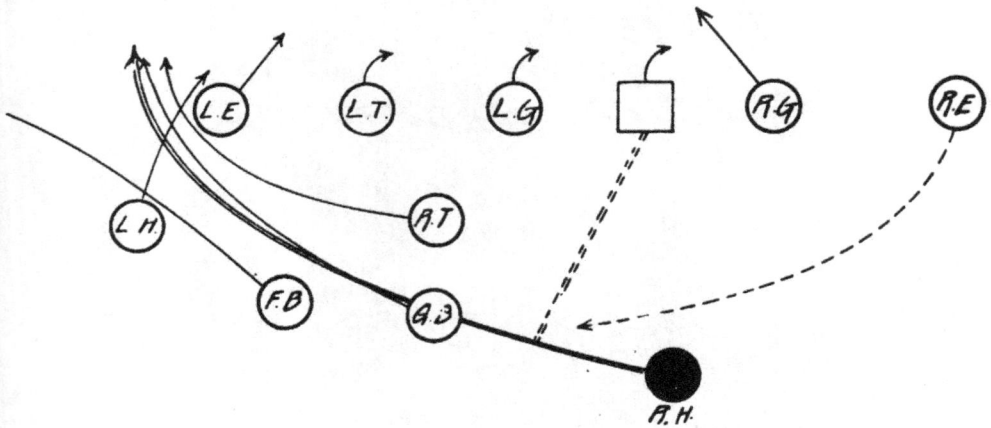

Direct Pass Formation—Right Half Back Run Around Left End.

In this play the half back takes the ball on a direct pass from cen er. To make it effective all the interference must get away quickly and move rapidly. This should be a much stronger play than the direct pass run by the quarter back. Center should be careful in his pass to right half, as the distance is a little longer than his usual pass.   He should pass it ahead of the half back so that he can receive it on the run.

Left Guard blocks to the right.

Right Guard breaks through and joins the runner.

Left Tackle blocks to the right.

Right Tackle follows left half back in the interference.

Left End boxes opposing tackle.

Right End follows around behind the runner.

Quarter Back follows right tackle in the interference.

Left Half Back blocks opposing defensive back.

Right Half Back is the runner.

Full Back blocks opposing end.

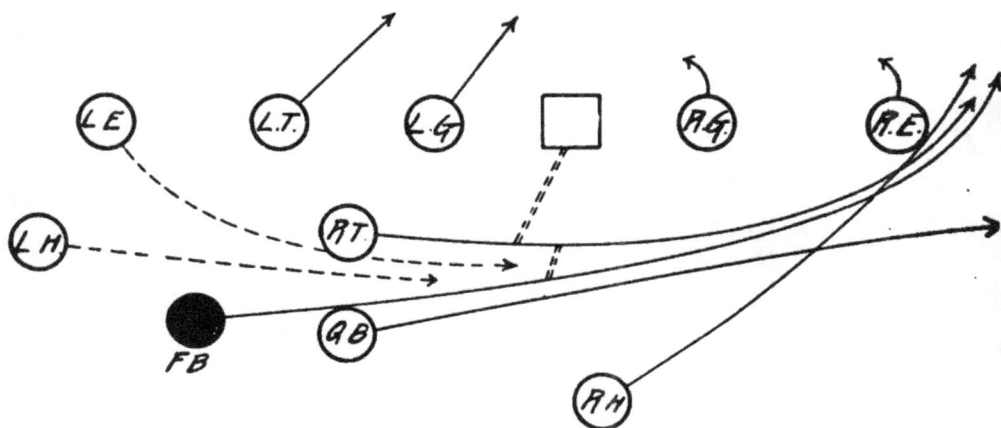

Direct Pass Formation—Double Pass—Right Tackle to Full Back.

This play to be used when opponents are shifting to stop the preceding play.

Center blocks to the left.

Left Guard breaks through.

Right Guard blocks to the left.

Left Tackle breaks through and joins the runner.

Right Tackle follows right half in the interference around right end.

Left End follows in the interference.

Right End boxes opposing tackle.

Quarter Back blocks opposing end.

Left Half Back assists the runner from the left side.

Right Half Back leads the interference and blocks the opposing half back.

Full Back is the runner.

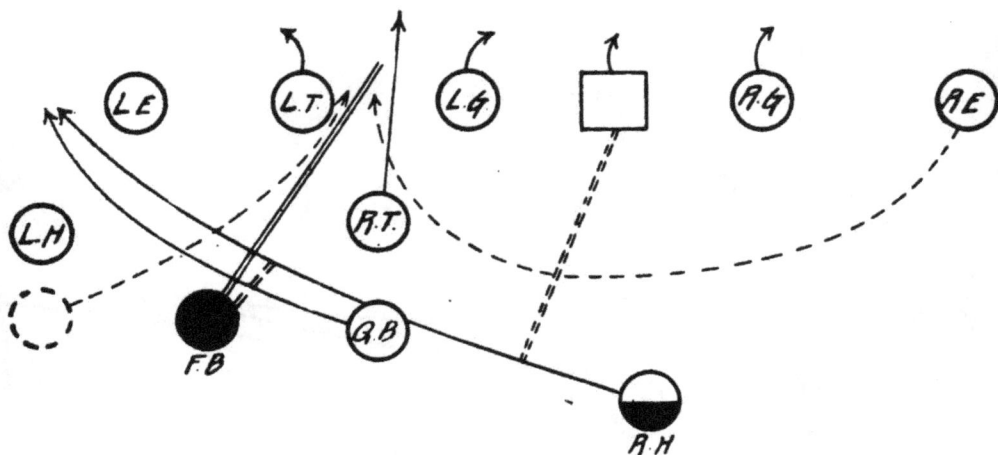

**Direct Pass Formation—Double Pass—Right Half Back
to Full Back.**

This is in the nature of a feint attack on left end for
a full back plunge through the line.

Center must be careful in making pass to right half back.

Left Guard blocks to the right.

Right Guard blocks to the right.

Left Tackle blocks to the left.

Right Tackle goes straight ahead and makes a hole for the
     runner.

Left End assists in blocking opposing tackle out.

Right End follows around and joins in the push.

Quarter Back leads a feint attack on left end.

Left Half Back, who has taken a position slightly behind
     his original position, hesitates a moment and then goes
     through on the left hip of the full back.

Right Half Back receives the ball from center on the run
     and passes it to the full back and follows the quarter
     back on around left end.

Full Back hesitates until he receives the ball and plunges
     through the line in the path of the right tackle.

Wing Shift Formation.—Ball passed directly to left half back.

Photo by Lyndon.

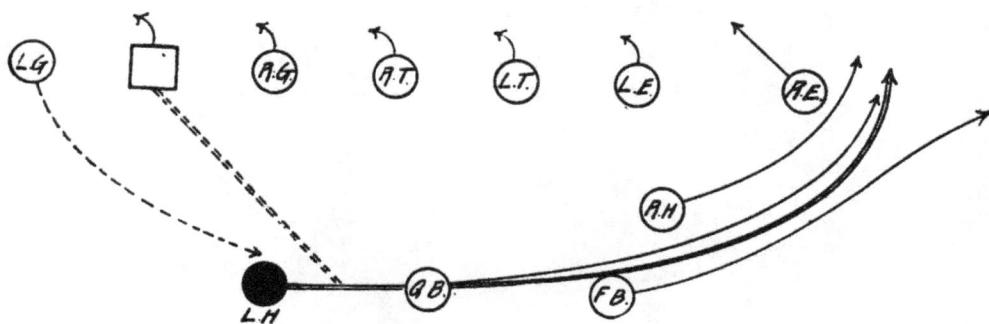

Wing Shift Formation—Direct Pass to Left Half Back.

Practically the entire team is shifted and the success of this play will depend almost entirely on lining up quickly and starting the play immediately. Do not give opponents time to take in the situation thoroughly.

Center must be careful in his pass, as it is a long, quick one.

Left Guard follows for safety man.

Right Guard blocks to the left.

Left Tackle blocks to the left.

Right Tackle blocks to the left.

Left End blocks to the left.

Right End blocks to the left.

Quarter Back follows right half back in the interference around right end.

Left Half Back takes the ball on a direct pass from center and follows quarter back.

Full Back blocks opposing right end.

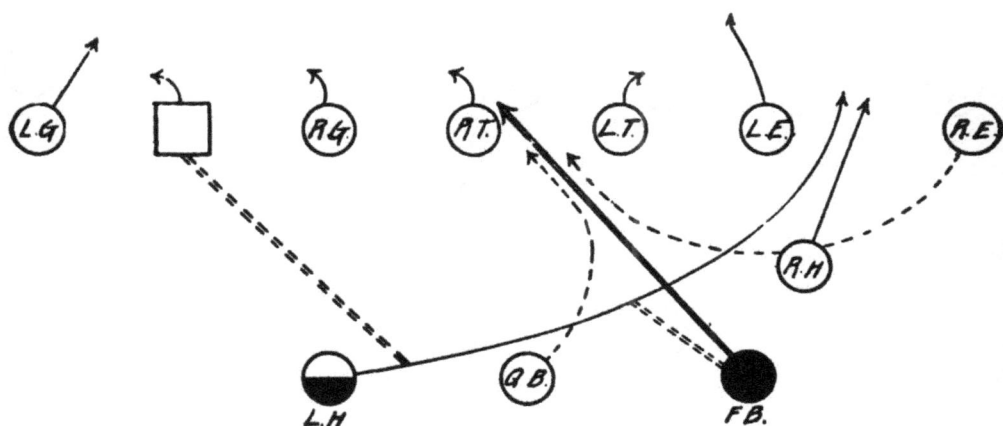

Wing Shift Formation—Double Pass—Left Half Back to Full Back.

This is a feint attack on right end with a full back plunge diagonally forward between the two tackles.

Center must watch out to make pass properly.

Left Guard goes through and blocks to the left.

Right Guard blocks to the left.

Left Tackle blocks to the right.

Right Tackle blocks to the left.

Left End assists right tackle in blocking to the right.

Right End comes around and assists the runner.

Quarter Back hesitates a moment, then assists the runner on the left hip.

Left Half Back receives the ball and passes it on the run to the full back.

Right Half Back makes a feint around right end, blocking anyone he can to the right.

Full Back after receiving the ball plunges between right and left tackle.

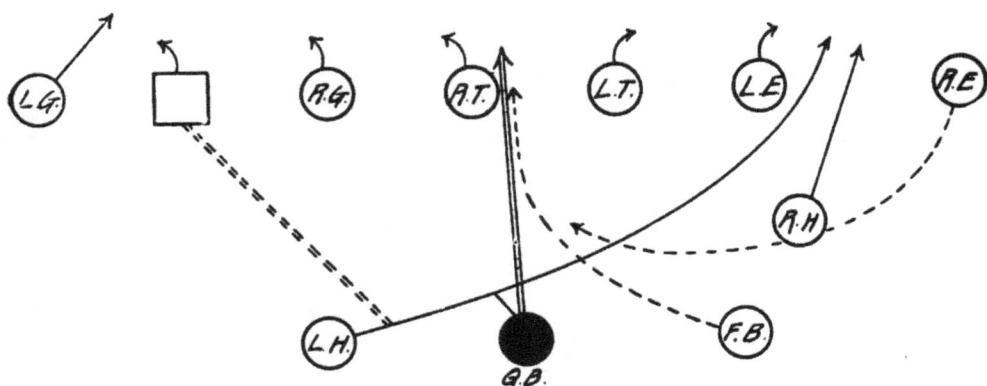

Wing Shift Formation—Double Pass—Left Half Back to Quarter Back.

The quarter back and right half back can change places, making the same formation exactly, so that the half back will be the one to plunge with the ball.

Center must pass the ball accurately.

Left Guard goes through and blocks to the left.

Right Guard blocks to the left.

Left Tackle blocks to the right.

Right Tackle blocks to the left.

Left End blocks to the right.

Right End hurries around and assists the runner.

Quarter Back, who has changed positions with the right half back, goes directly forward and blocks to the right.

Left Half Back receives the ball and passes it to the right half back and follows quarter back through right end, carrying out the feint attack.

Right Half Back when he receives the ball goes straight ahead between left and right tackle.

Full Back pushes the runner through from behind.

Photo by Lyndon.

Formation for a punt or for a fake kick.—Ends may go down under kick from a position close to tackle or out farther, depending on the action of the opposing ends or men selected to block him. The kicker should see that all his blocking is in the proper position before asking for the ball from center.

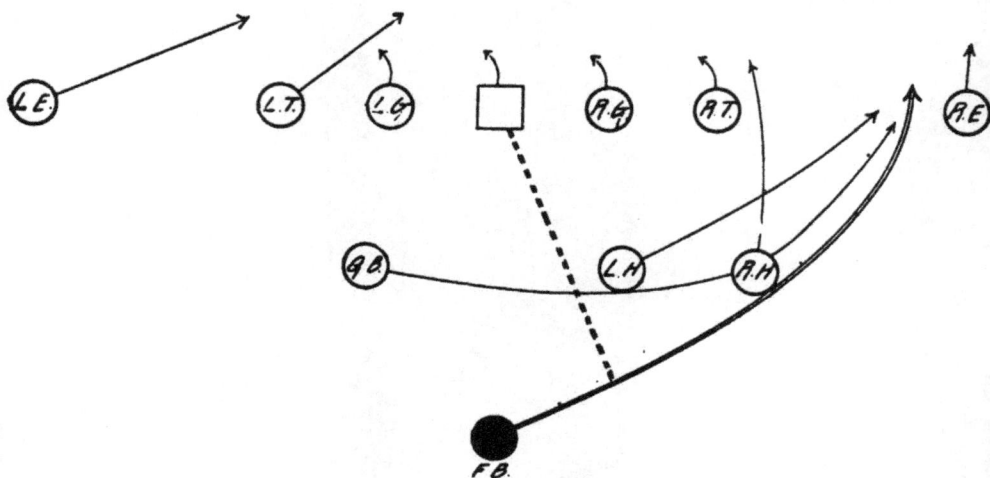

Fake Kick—Full Back Run.

The success of this play will depend largely in deceiving opponents into believing it is a real kick. All the men in the interference must do their duty.

Center in making the pass should make it so that the full back will get it on the run. This will help the play along very much.

Left Guard blocks to the left.

Right Guard blocks to the left.

Left Tackle blocks to the left and goes through to block opposing full back.

Right Tackle blocks to the left.

Left End goes ahead and blocks any of the opposing backs he can.

Right End blocks opposing end.

Quarter Back gets into the interference for the full back.

Left Half Back leads the interference for the full back.

Right Half Back blocks opposing defensive back.

Full Back is the runner.

Photo by Lyndon.

Formation for the defense against a punt or fake kick.—Two men in back-field to receive kick; man at quarter ready for any fake through line or around ends; ends ready for fake or to block opposing ends going down under punt; line to go through and block kick.

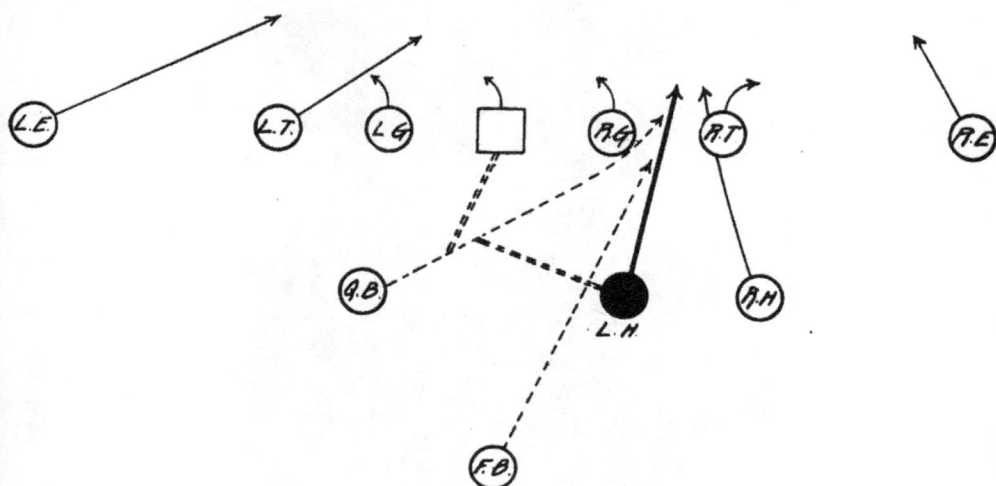

Fake Kick—Left Half Back Straight Through.

This play can be used with effect when the opposing line is playing wide so as to get through to block the kick or to stop a big kick around end.

Center passes to quarter and then blocks to the left.

Left Guard blocks to the left.

Right Guard blocks to the left.

Left Tackle goes through, blocks defensive quarter back.

Right Tackle blocks to the right.

Left End goes across and joins the runner.

Right End blocks opposing end.

Quarter Back receives the ball from center on the run and passes it to the left half back.

Left Half Back hesitates a second, receives the ball and then goes directly ahead.

Right Half Back assists right tackle in blocking out. ·

Full Back follows from behind.

Regular formation on defense.—Ends should not be too wide from tackles.

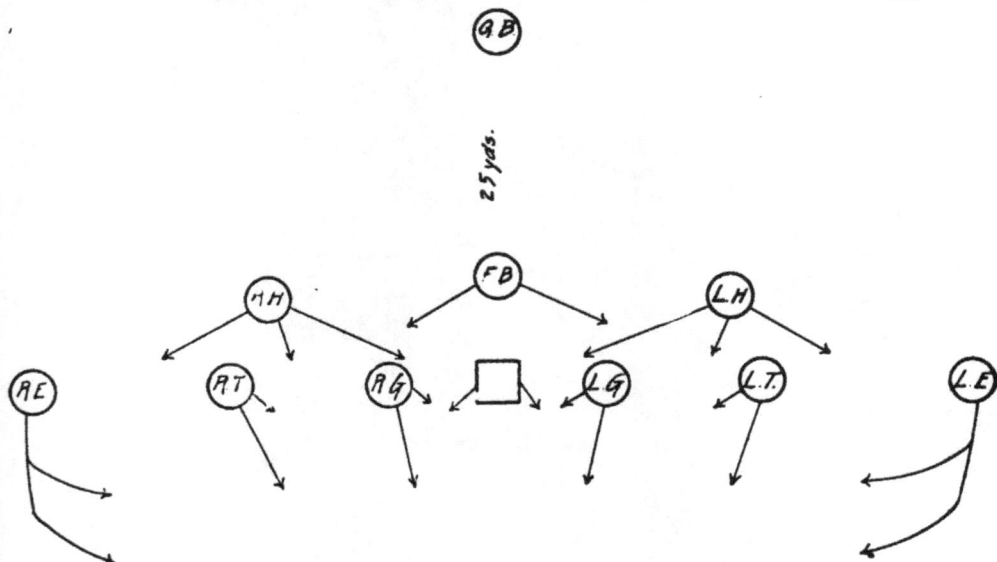

Defensive Formation—Regular.

The two ends should play close to the tackle, about three yards out; should charge ahead instantly with the snap of the ball, turning in quickly if play is directed at the line, but keeping well outside of all opponents' interference.

The two tackles must play wide enough so that they cannot be easily boxed by the opposing ends, yet not so wide that they can be easily thrown out. Use hands freely. Remember the end is the dangerous man.

The center should play a little higher and freer than either of the guards and he must be in position to do tackling on either side of center, or in fact along the entire line.

The three defensive backs must tackle everywhere. Wherever the runner is, there they must be.

The defensive quarter back should judge his distance behind the line by the direction of the wind and the strength of the opposing kicker. He must never be drawn in too close.

Defense.—Shifted to meet a shifting attack, such as tackle-over cr tackle-back formations.

Photo Lydon 105

QB

25 yds.

FB   L.H

R.E   R.H   R.T   R.G   Opp C   L.G   L.T   L.E

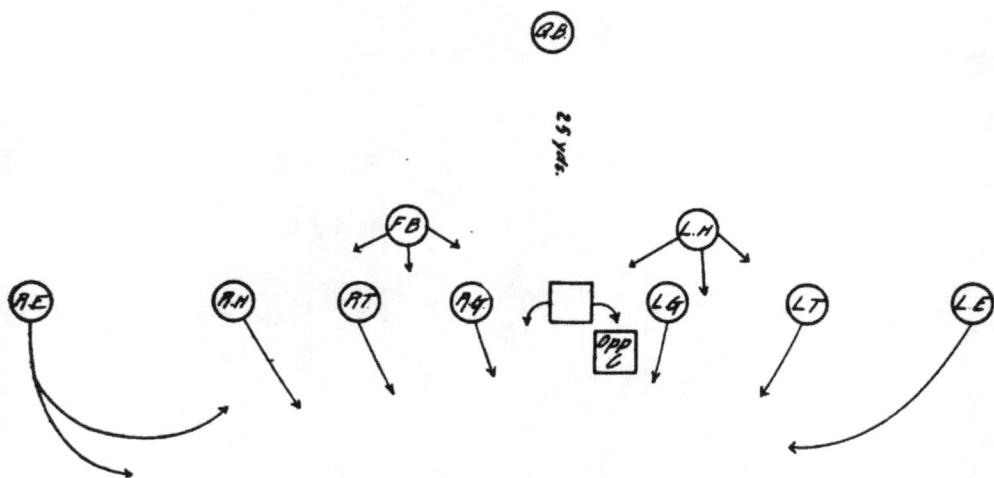

Defensive Formation—Line and Back-Field Shift.

This formation is used to meet the various tackle-back plays and tackle over on the line plays. The halftone illustration on the opposite page shows the position the men should assume just before the opponents snap the ball. In the diagram above the opposing center is shown, so that the relative position of the defensive linemen is shown as compared with the offensive linemen; the entire line on defense is shifted a half a man to the right. The right half back has gone up on the line with the right tackle. The defensive quarter back, which is being played by the full back, and the left half back have shifted their positions to the right. This would be the position taken by the team if the opposing side were using right tackle back or right tackle over on the line. The men would shift to just the opposite position should the opposing attack demand it.

Defense.—Ends in close to charge and break interference immediately.

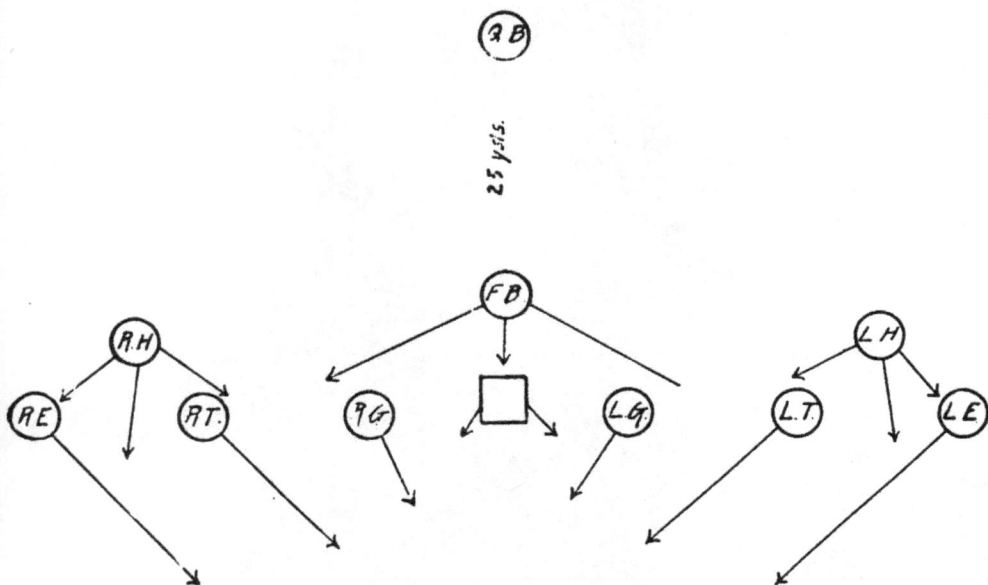

Defensive Formation—Ends In.

This diagram shows what is commonly known as the Pennsylvania defense. The ends are played in very close to tackle and sent immediately into the opposing interference to break it up or tackle the runner. They will meet the interference before it is under much headway and will often be successful in spoiling the play behind the line. If the ends do not get the runner he will usually be left without interference and can be easily tackled by one of the defensive backs.

The two tackles play wide, but are driven in toward the center by a shove from the defensive backs.

The men are supposed to play along the lines as shown in the diagram. The halftone illustration on the opposite page shows the position the men should assume just before the ball is put in play by the opponents.

GENERALSHIP

THE CAPTAIN

Second only to the judicious selection and thorough training of a football team is the acquisition of a capable captain, for no matter how well the eleven may be qualified for its work, individually and as a team, its efforts will be barren of success unless the men are ably led on the field.

No matter how well disciplined and equipped for battle an army may be, if its general is cowardly or lacking in foresight and strategy, its efforts will yield only defeat. The same is true of a football team and its campaign, for the captain is the commander of the eleven and on his ability and on the influence of his personality depends largely whether his team is to emerge from its game in glorious victory or in disappointing defeat.

No player should be selected to act as captain who is not a leader in every sense of the word. He should be a player of the very highest individual ability in the first place, for, if he lacks ability to perform his own part in the play, scant will be the confidence which his men will place in him and his commands. He should be able at all times to set an example which his comrades must exert themselves to the utmost to follow. His spirit and enthusiasm must be contagious, for the team will play in exactly the fashion in which it is led, and carelessness or indifference in a leader will be mirrored in every movement of his team. The captain must be a perfect judge of human nature and must be able to meet each crisis as it comes with a fearlessness and aggressiveness which will communicate themselves to every member of his team.

If possible, the captain should by all means be the quarter back of the team, for it is from this position that the duties of field leader can best be performed.

The football captain should be a man who has the ability and disposition to make a close study of his own men as well as of his opponents. He should enter each game prepared in advance in the minutest detail possible and equipped with a knowledge immediately available when called for. His team has been prepared to the best of the ability of its instructors, and when it takes the field to do battle, when·the time for action arrives, the captain must realize that the situation now rests with him. He it is who must execute the plan of play that has been arranged. Is his own team strong in one particular, he must be prompt and ready to make use of that strength in the way that will prove most effective. Is there a weakness in the opposing eleven, he must be quick to discover it and must emphasize it by so directing his play that the strength of his own team and the weakness of the opponents are combined to bring victory to the eleven which he is leading.

Summed up, the football captain must be a good general. In adversity he must be prepared to encourage his men to still further efforts, while rapidly evolving a plan which will meet conditions that may not have been foreseen. Even the elements, wind, sun and weather, must be brought into an alliance with his efforts. He must be an adept in field tactics. He must justify his selection as field leader by always doing the right thing in the right place. He owes it to his men, and they, in turn, owe him an obedience which, when given, needs only the addition of general knowledge and ability to make victory over any

team of equal and even superior prowess, but less skillfully
led, an absolute certainty.

LOOKING FORWARD, OR THINGS THAT SHOULD BE KNOWN BEFORE THE GAME

The condition of the field is an important factor in
every football contest. Knowledge of the gridiron's individual peculiarities is just as essential to the football captain as is thorough familiarity with his battle ground to
a commander of an army. Some time before the game the
coach and captain should go over the field carefully and
note its condition. It may slope toward the end or the
side. It may have good footing in parts. It may be partly
sod and partly bare. It may just have rained or snowed
and the effect of the weather on the different parts of the
field may be vastly different. Every condition must be
minutely noted, for the commander must maneuver his
forces along plans that will take every possible advantage
of existing conditions.

The sun and wind are important factors that enter into
the playing of the game and their influence on the play
must be carefully noted and considered. On their direction
depends largely the style of kick to be employed and the
number of times kicking should be resorted to.

If the ground is soft from the nature of the soil or
from rain or snow, great care should be taken that all the
players' shoes are well cleated. No one can play the game
unless he has a good and secure footing. Any player who
has an injury should have it well protected by proper bandages or padding, this being especially important on a field
that is hard or frozen.

The captain should know his own men, their strength
and weakness as a whole and individuals. This can all

be acquired during the practice season by noting carefully the playing of the team and men at all times.

The coach, captain and quarter back should go over the plan of the game to be played. This should be done in detail the day before the game. At this meeting all data concerning the players of the opposing team must be considered. Their make-up and their possibilities, singly and as a team, both on the offense and defense, should govern largely the plan of campaign to be decided upon. Knowledge of this sort can best be gained by actual observation of the opponents in action against some other team.

Ground rules should be agreed upon where any obstacles are likely to interfere with the playing of the game. Many gridirons have the stands or fences where they will interfere with plays and kicks that go out of bounds and in goal. An understanding beforehand will settle any difficulty that may arise later.

THE OFFENSE

It would be simply foolish even to attempt to lay out a general plan by which a football game should be played. One universal feature of the game is the fact that it cannot be worked out very well before the actual conditions arise on the field. Football cannot be learned by rule. Only a general idea can be offered of what the leader must keep in mind during the game,—a few suggestions that will assist him to make the proper moves at the right time and place.

In preparation for each game, the style of offense to be decided upon must depend largely on the style, strength and weakness of the opponents' defense. But this much is certain,—the offense should include such a varied attack that some of the plays will be effective against any style

OFFENSE.

Defensive Goal.

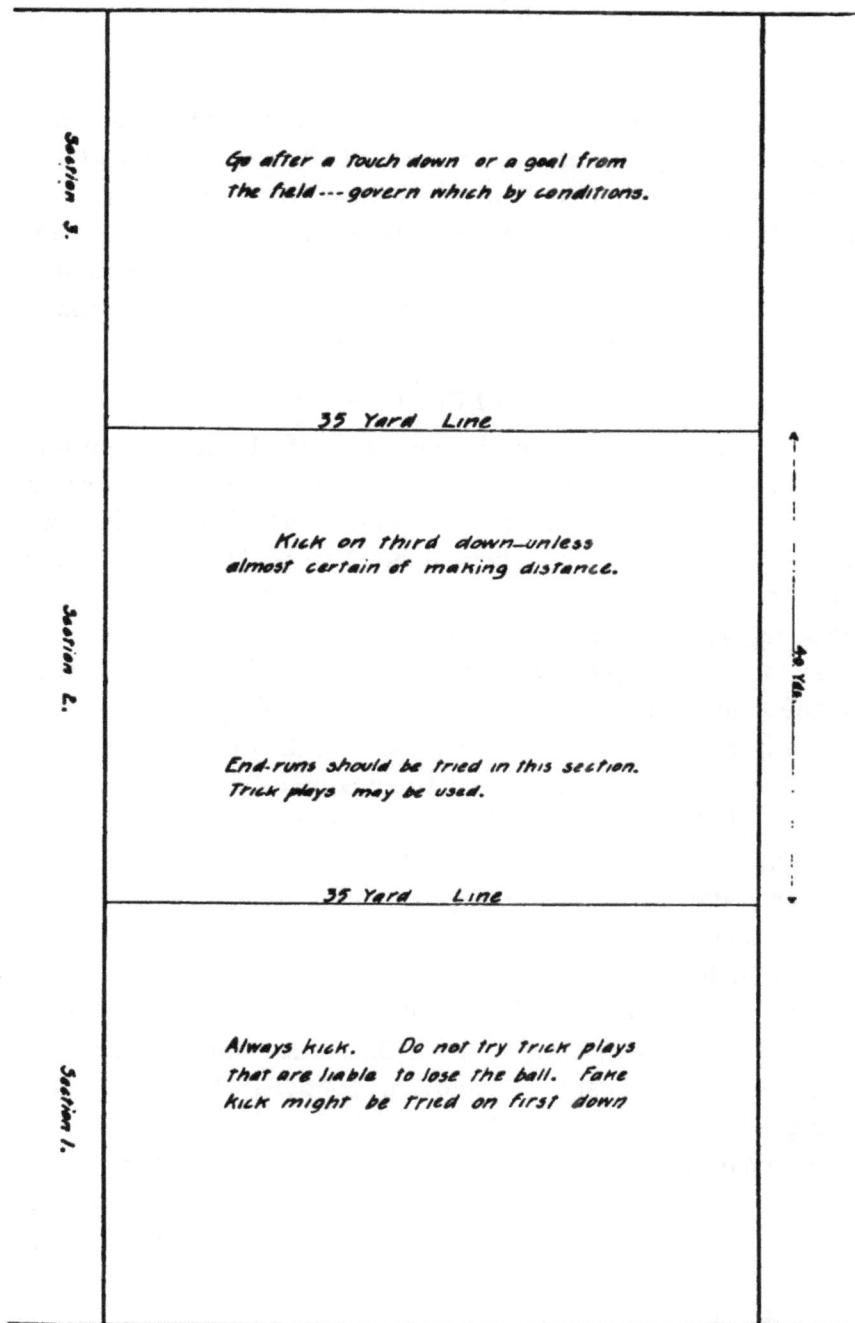

Go after a touch down or a goal from the field --- govern which by conditions.

35 Yard Line

Kick on third down — unless almost certain of making distance.

End-runs should be tried in this section. Trick plays may be used.

35 Yard Line

Always kick. Do not try trick plays that are liable to lose the ball. Fake kick might be tried on first down

Section 3.

Section 2.

Section 1.

40 Yds.

Offensive Goal.

Suggestions to aid in selection of plays on offense in different sections of the field.

of defense the opponents may offer. The game must not be played to suit the opponents, but should be so planned as to take every possible advantage of their weakness. How often it occurs that a team plays into the hands of its opponents, shoots the ball into its pocket, as it were, and wonders why the play fails to gain. The modern offensive game, to be as effective as it should, is one that is made up of a variety of plays and different formations.

THE OFFENSE NO. 2

The main attack should be diversified and deceptive, but the deceptive feature of the attack should be more in the nature of straight football than trick plays. It may feint at one point and then strike the real blow at some other point. On the offense the opponents must be kept guessing as to the nature and kind of attack. This is very important if the play is to gain ground. The main object of the team on the offense is to score—to carry the ball over the opponents' goal. All the attack should have this end in view. The plays must be executed with such force, speed and determination that they cannot be resisted.

Sometimes it is good policy to keep up a consistent attack at some point in the opposing line and then suddenly shift it back to some other place, after the enemy has drawn in its men to stop the play at the original point. This does not mean that the attack must be limited to a small number of plays, for punts, fake kicks, line plunges, sudden shifts in the offensive formation, followed by end runs, should all be included in the general policy.

Straight football should form the principal attack, and punting should be considered an important part. Do not rely on trick plays. They will very rarely gain ground against good teams and the weaker ones can be easily defeated anyhow.

THE OFFENSE NO. 3

Kicking is an important part of the offense. The team that does not have a good punter in the game and one or two in reserve is seriously handicapped. Just when and where to kick are decisions that must be governed largely by the strength of the two teams and the condition of the wind and weather. Again, can you out-kick the opposing team, and what is your ability to hold your opponents when they have secured the ball from a punt? If the opponents' back-field men are poor at catching, kick often. When punting from near the sideline, care must be taken that the ball does not go outside too soon in flight. If punting from near the sideline, do not kick too far toward the other side, as the opposing backs will have a great chance to run the ball back along the side of the field that is little protected. The punt should always be high enough to permit the ends to go down the field with the ball to tackle the runner or get the ball in case of a fumble.

OFFENSE IN DIFFERENT SECTIONS OF THE FIELD

Section 1. When the opponents are inside your own 35-yard line, there is always much danger of their scoring either by a touchdown or a goal from the field. Strive to prevent in every way possible the enemy's securing possession of the ball in this territory. The general policy should be to kick on first down or just as soon as you secure the ball. The danger in rushing the ball in Section 1 is that a fumble may occur and the ball be secured by the opponents. Keep the play out and beyond the 35-yard line. This is a good section of the field to try a fake kick or trick play of some kind on first down. Under no conditions, however, try a play in which there is any likelihood of a fumble.

...sitions of the men just before ball is passed. The line must hold together.

In kicking from this territory the full back must use great care in getting his kick off and in playing it so that the opponents can not make a fair catch. Care in this respect is especially necessary if the kicker punts from near or behind his own goal line. The center must be careful in his pass to the full back and the full back should be slightly farther back from the center than he usually is for the kick.

Section 2. Section 2, or the center of the field, is the great battle-ground of the game. It is here that all the tricks and maneuvers of football are put into play. Every method is tried, likely to carry the ball toward the opponents' goal. In this section the punting is more frequent. Kicking should be resorted to on the third down in the middle section, if there is any possibility of losing the ball. If the wind is at your back, punt frequently, especially if you can out-kick your opponents, for this gain on the exchange will gradually bring you nearer the coveted goal line.

The plays should be so directed that the team is not brought in too near the sideline, and the point of attack thus practically limited to one side of the line.

A kick from this section of the field should be so directed that the ball will go out of bounds near the goal line or so that it will stop near the goal line and not go in goal. If the ball goes in goal the opponents will fall on it for a touch-back, and they will be permitted to kick out from the 25-yard line instead of being forced to take a kick from scrimmage on or near their own goal line.

Section 3. When the team has once crossed the opponents' 35-yard line, the attack should grow stronger and more determined. Every inch counts now and every member of the eleven should get in with all his power. The selection of plays is very important and only the ones that are strongest and best should be attemped. If the opponents play close in the line and bring in their back-field, do not be afraid to use the plays that go outside of tackle, and even farther out if the end comes in as close as he often does. This does not mean, however, that you must try a wide end run.

It is not hard to score a goal from the field at any point inside the 35-yard line. If conditions arise on the third down that are liable to result in the loss of the ball, then try a goal from the field either by a place-kick or drop-kick, depending, of course, on the play for which the team is better fitted.

DEFENSE

The style of defense used depends largely on the style of attack of the opponents. The position on the field of play will govern largely the disposition of men and their duties on the defense. The conditions of the ground must not be overlooked. When the ground is wet and slippery it is almost impossible to run the ends, who can then be played in close to the tackles and the tackles in more toward the guards.

The modern system of defense receives almost as much attention as the offense. The great variety of attack now in use in the different schools and colleges of the country demands that the defense be arranged for the best manner of stopping the attack. Under the chapter on "Defense" will be shown and explained the best and most effective formations for defense now used. There should be a system of signals for the defense just as much as there is for the attack.

The defense against kicks and the duties of the individuals and the team as a whole are fully explained under the head of "Punting."

A FEW "HURRY UPS"

Hurry up.

Hurry up and be the first man to line up.

-Hurry all the time ; football is not a slow or lazy man's game.

Hurry up ; football is a game of hurry, hurry, hurry.

Hurry up if you are behind in any play. Then is the time you need most to hurry.

Hurry up and get into every play. Football is played by eleven men. Spectators are not wanted on the field ; their place is in the grand stand.

Hurry up and be the first man down the field on a punt or kick-off.

— Hurry up and help your own runner with the ball ; never let him go it alone.

Hurry up and follow the ball. No one can play the game unless he is with the ball all the time.

Hurry up and fall on every fumble, either by your own side or an opponent. This is very important.

— Hurry up and block your man hard when you should block.

Hurry up when given the ball for a gain. You must hurry or the opponents will be all over you in an instant.

Hurry up and learn the signals. You cannot play a fast game unless you know them instantly.

— Hurry up and learn to control your temper. If you cannot do this you had better quit the game.

Hurry up when you are about to be tackled. Put on more "go." Don't slow up, for this is the time of all others when you need all your speed.

Hurry up and do not talk unless you are the captain or the quarter back. You are in the game to act.

Hurry up and do as your coach and trainer advise you. If you know more about the game than they do, it is time for you to quit.

Hurry up and always block your inside man if you are playing on the line of scrimmage.

Hurry up and get versatile. Do not be a machine player in your individual position.

Hurry up when meeting an interference and go into it low. It is so much more easily stopped.

Hurry up and stop every play of the opponents before it gets started. Tear through and get the runner behind the opponents' line. Never wait for him.

Hurry up and tackle the runner. Do not expect anyone else to do it. See to it that you throw him toward his own goal.

Hurry up and score in the first few minutes of the game, before your opponents realize what is going on.

Hurry up and line up the instant that the ball is dead. The delay of one man in taking his place will completely ruin fast play.

Hurry up and line up. The next play cannot start until all are ready.

Hurry up and play football. Do not slug, for slugging prevents any man from playing the team play that he should. You will be kept busy performing your part in the game.

Hurry up even if you are tired; do not slow down. If you cannot stand the pace, get yourself into better condition. Football is a strenuous game.

Hurry up and master the rules of the game. How do you expect to play the game properly if you are not familiar with the rules? Lots of company in this fault is no excuse for you.

Hurry up and be on time for practice and all other meetings of the players. If you cannot be there promptly, turn in your suit. You do not have the proper interest.

Hurry up and obey the decisions of the officials. They and not you have been selected to run the game.

Looking forward—the future half back.

FOOT BALL RULES

RE-ARRANGED WITH SUGGESTIONS

The rules following have been re-arranged so that the player can easily see who has charge of each section and what the penalty is for violating the same. A few suggestions are also added to call attention to some points that are often overlooked. The rules are very important and a close study by every one who wishes to play the game will do as much to prepare them to play the game properly as will anything else. There is entirely too much ignorance in regard to football rules.

These are the official football rules for 1905, reprinted from Spalding's Official Football Guide, by special permission.

THE OFFICIALS

DUTIES OF REFEREE

In making his decisions the Referee must recognize and allow precedence to any penalty inflicted by the umpire for a foul.

The Referee's decisions are final upon all points not specified under the duties of the Umpire.

The Referee shall see that the ball is properly put in play, and he is judge of its position and progress.

He is judge of forward passes, of interference with the snap-back, and of the advance of the ball by the player who first receives it from the snapper-back when the ball is put in play from a scrimmage (Rule 16, *a* and *e*), and offenses under Rule 18, *c*.

At the beginning of a game and in every case after time has been taken out, he shall ascertain from each captain that his team is ready, before ordering play to begin.

He is sole authority for the score of the game and is judge of forfeiture of the game under the rules.

The Referee may appeal to both the Umpire and Linesman for testimony upon all points within his jurisdiction.

The Referee must volunteer testimony to the Umpire concerning infringement of Rule 27 (c and f).

DUTIES OF UMPIRE

The Umpire is judge of the conduct of the players, and his decision is final regarding such fouls as are not specifically placed within the jurisdiction of the Referee.

The Umpire is judge of charging, and of the positions of players whenever the ball is put in play.

He may appeal to both the Referee and Linesman for testimony in cases of fouls seen by them, and it shall be their duty to volunteer testimony concerning violations of Rule 27 (c and f).

NOTE—Captains and players, however, may not appeal to the Referee or Linesman for their testimony upon the points just mentioned.

The Umpire shall not signal with his horn or bell, except to declare a foul committed.

Whenever the Umpire notices or is informed by the Referee or Linesman that a substitute or any other person not participating in the game is coaching, he shall immediately exclude the offender for the remainder of the game from the neighborhood of the field of play; *i. e.*, send the offender behind the ropes or fence surrounding the field of play.

Furthermore, he shall exact the penalty as provided in
Rule 28.

*NOTE—The Referee should use a whistle to indicate
cessation of play on downs, fair catches and fouls, and the
Umpire (and Linesman) should use a horn or a bell of some
kind, distinguishable from the Referee's whistle, to indicate
that a foul has been committed.*

DUTIES OF LINESMAN

The Linesman shall, under the supervision of the Referee, mark the distances gained or lost in the progress of
the play.

He shall remain on the side-lines and be provided with
two assistants, who shall remain outside the field of play
and who shall use, in measuring distance, the rope or chain
mentioned in Note under Rule 1 (*d*).

The Linesman shall, under the direction of the Referee,
also keep the time, and he should use a stop-watch in so
doing. He should start his watch not when the Referee
blows his whistle, but when the ball is put in play.

The Linesman must penalize a side for the ends being
off-side on a kick, for tripping of ends after a kick, and for
roughing the full-back. It should be his special duty to be
in position to see that the ends are on-side when the ball
is put in play in a scrimmage. In case the Linesman gives
a decision against one side and the Umpire against the
other on the same play, the penalties being other than disqualification, the ball shall be brought back to the point
where it was put in play and played over again, the number of the down and the point to be gained for first down
remaining the same. In case of disqualification by either
official, at any time, the disqualification shall stand. In

case the Linesman and Umpire each signal a foul against the same side during the same scrimmage (unnecessary roughness excepted) only one penalty shall be given, viz.: that for the foul committed first. In case it is impossible to say which foul occurred first the penalty shall be exacted only for the foul noted by the Umpire.

In the above cases a foul called by the Referee shall be judged the same as if called by the Linesman. That is, in case more than one foul is called on the same play, one foul being against one side and the other against the other, the ball shall be brought back as stated above. In case more than one foul is called upon the same side and it is impossible to say which foul occurred first, then only one penalty shall be exacted, a decision by the Referee taking precedence over that of the Umpire and that of the Umpire over that of the Linesman.

The Linesman shall notify the captains of the time remaining for play, not more than 10 nor less than 5 minutes before the end of each half.

NOTE—There is no objection to the Linesman giving approximate time to an inquiring captain at any time during the game. He may not, however, be asked for this time more than 3 times within the last 5 minutes of the half.

EQUIPMENT, OFFICIALS, ETC.

RULE 1.

REFEREE HAS JURISDICTION OF EACH SECTION.

Field.

(*a*) The game shall be played upon a rectangular field, 330 feet in length and 160 feet in width, enclosed by heavy white lines marked in lime upon the ground. The lines at the two ends shall be termed goal lines. The side lines shall extend beyond their points of intersection with the goal line. The goal shall be placed in the middle of each goal line, and shall consist of two upright posts exceeding 20 feet in height and placed 18 feet 6 inches apart, with horizontal cross-bar 10 feet from the ground.

Players.

(*b*) The game shall be played by two teams of eleven men each.

Officials.

(*c*) The officials of the game shall be a Referee, an Umpire and a Linesman.

Ball.

(*d*) The foot ball used shall be of leather, enclosing an inflated rubber bladder. The ball shall have the shape of a prolate spheroid.

NOTE—It is desirable to have two stop-watches for the time-keepers, a whistle for the referee and a horn or a bell of some kind for the umpire, in order to distinguish his call from that of the referee. It is also desirable to have the field marked off with white lines every 5 yards, parallel to the goal line, for measuring the 5 yards to be gained in 3 downs, and to provide two light poles about 6 feet in length and connected at the lower ends by a stout cord or chain exactly 5 yards long. In addition to this the field should be marked off with white lines 5 yards apart, parallel to side lines, in order to assist the officials in judging whether the first man who receives the ball crosses the scrimmage line a sufficient distance from where the ball was put in play. Instead of having those lines continuous it may be sufficient to mark only the cross lines above named at the points where they are crossed by these lines.

In measuring, the forward point of the ball, in its position when declared dead, not its center, shall be taken as the determining point.

DEFINITION OF TERMS

RULE 2.

REFEREE HAS JURISDICTION OF EACH SECTION.

METHODS OF KICKING THE BALL.

Drop-kick.

(a) A *Drop-kick* is made by letting the ball drop from the hands and kicking it the instant it rises from the ground.

SUGGESTION.—The players should remember that if the goal is missed the opponents may either make a touchback or run with the ball, so the forwards and the ends should be on the lookout and force the opponents to make a touchback or stop them just after they have crossed the goal line. If the drop-kick is tried after a fair catch, all are on-side and can go and secure the ball, if the goal is missed, whether it has been touched by an opponent or not.

Place-kick.

(b) A *Place-kick* is made by kicking the ball after it has been placed on the ground.

SUGGESTION.—The player must remember that the same conditions govern an attempt at goal by a place-kick as by a drop-kick.

Punt.

(c) A *Punt* is made by letting the ball drop from the hands and kicking it before it touches the ground.

Kick-off.

(d) A *Kick-off* is a place-kick from the center of the field of play, and cannot score a goal. (Rule 8.)

SUGGESTION.—All are on-side at the kick-off and any one can secure the ball after it has gone ten yards, even before it has been touched by an opponent. If the ball is kicked in goal, go down and fall on it for a touchdown or prevent the opponents from running it back. Be sure that

Place Kicking.—Showing how to make the kick.

the ball was called down by the player or dead by the referee before it is brought back on the field of play.

Kick-out.

(e) A *Kick-out* is a drop-kick, place-kick or punt made by a player of the side which has made a safety or a touchback.

SUGGESTION.—When kicking out from the ten or twenty-five-yard line on a kick-out, everyone is on-side and can go and get the ball or interfere with a fair catch. The side kicking out can kick from any point behind the ten or twenty-five-yard line. They should do this and take advantage of any wind or field conditions, being careful not to kick the ball so the opponents can make a fair catch and have a good position to kick a goal from the field.

Free-kick.

(f) A *Free-kick* is a term used to designate any kick when the opponents are restrained by rule from advancing beyond a certain point before the ball is put in play.

NOTE—Under a Free-kick are included Kick-off (Rule 2, d), Kick-out (Rule 2, e), Punt-out (Rules 5 and 25); Kick from a Fair Catch (Rule 7), and Place-kick for Goal after a touchdown (Rules 4 (a) and 25). Any player of the side having the Free-kick may put the ball in play.

RULE 3.

REFEREE HAS JURISDICTION OF EACH SECTION.

Out of Bounds.

(a) The ball is *Out of Bounds* when it touches the ground on or outside the side line or side line extended, or when any part of the player who holds the ball touches the ground on or outside the side line or side line extended.

SUGGESTION.—When a player is running with the ball and is tackled, or about to be tackled, he should by all means carry the ball across the side-line or out of bounds. This will give his team the advantage of bringing it in fifteen yards instead of being forced into a scrimmage near the side-line.

(*b*) If the ball is kicked so that it goes out of bounds before crossing the opponents' goal line, it shall belong to the opponents at the point where it crossed the side line. If, however, it strikes any player who is on side and then goes out of bounds, it shall belong to the player who first obtains possession of it.

RULE 4.

Referee Has Jurisdiction of Each Section.

Touchdown.

(*a*) A *Touchdown* is made when the ball in possession of a player is declared dead by the referee, any part of it being on, over or behind the opponents' goal line.

(*b*) The point where the touchdown is marked, however, is not where the ball is carried across the line but where the ball is fairly held or called "down."

NOTE—If the ball is carried across the extension of the side line it is at once dead, and the touchdown is marked at the point where the side line crosses the goal line.

Touchback.

(*c*) A *Touchback* is made when the ball in possession of a player guarding his own goal is declared dead by the referee, any part of it being on, over or behind the goal line, provided the impetus which sent it to or across the line was given by an opponent. The referee shall declare the ball dead when the player in possession of the ball cries "down," or touches it down, or as provided for in Rule 20.

SUGGESTION.—A touchback is always made when a player touches the ball down in his own goal, the force which put it in goal having come from an opponent.

Safety.

(*d*) A *Safety* is made when the ball in the possession of a player guarding his own goal is declared dead by the referee, any part of it being on, over or behind the goal line, provided the impetus which caused it to pass from outside the goal to or behind the goal line was given by the side defending the goal. Such impetus could come: (1) from a kick, pass, snap-back or fumble by one of the player's own side; (2) from a kick which bounded back from an opponent; (3) in case a player carrying the ball is forced back, provided the ball was not declared dead by the referee before the line was reached or crossed.

A safety is also made when a player of the side in possession of the ball commits a foul which would give the ball to the opponents behind the offender's goal line; also when the ball, kicked by a man behind his goal line, crosses the side line extended behind the goal line.

RULE 5.

Referee Has Jurisdiction.

Punt-out.

A *Punt-out* is a punt made by a player of the side which has made a touchdown to another of his own side for a fair catch. (Rule 7.)

Suggestion.—See Rule 25, Section (*b*).

RULE 6.

Referee Has Jurisdiction.

Scrimmage.

(*a*) A *Scrimmage* takes place when the holder of the ball places it upon the ground and puts it in play by kicking it forward or snapping it back. The scrimmage does not end until the ball is again declared dead.

The ball is always put in play from a scrimmage, except in cases where other specific provision is made by the rules.

NOTE:—Snapping the ball means putting it back by means of hand or foot with one quick or continuous motion from its position on the ground.

Suggestion.—The defensive center must always be on the alert and watch that the opposing center does not have an opportunity to put the ball in play by kicking it through his position.

Referee Has Jurisdiction.

Feint to Snap the Ball.

(*b*) If, after the snapper-back has taken his position, he should voluntarily move the ball as if to snap it, whether he withholds it altogether or only momentarily, the ball is in play, and the scrimmage has begun.

Umpire Has Jurisdiction.

Snapper-back Off-side.

(*c*) When snapping the ball back, the player so doing must be on-side, the hand or foot used in snapping the ball excepted. (Rule 10.)

Referee Has Jurisdiction.

(*d*) If any player of the side in possession of the ball other than the snapper-back makes any deliberate attempt, by a false start or otherwise, to draw the opponents off-side, the ball, if then snapped, shall not be regarded as in play nor the scrimmage as begun.

RULE 7.

Referee Has Jurisdiction (except as relates to interference, throwing catcher, and position of players, of which umpire has jurisdiction).

Penalty.—If a player who has an opportunity of making a fair catch (Rule 7) is unlawfully obstructed by an opponent who is off-side and thus prevented from catching the ball, or if a player who has heeled a fair catch is thrown to the ground (unless he has advanced beyond his mark) his side shall have the choice of two penalties, viz.:

1. They may receive 15 yards, in which case they must put the ball in play by a scrimmage; or,

2. They may receive 5 yards, in which case they must put the ball in play by a punt, drop-kick or place-kick.

Fair Catch.

(*a*) A *Fair catch* consists in catching the ball after it has been kicked by one of the opponents and before it touches the ground, or in similarily catching a punt-out by another of the catcher's own side, provided the player, while making the catch, makes a mark with his heel and takes not more than one step thereafter. It is not a fair catch if the ball, after the kick, was touched by another of his side before the catch. Opponents who are off-side shall not interfere in any way with a player who has an opportunity to make a fair catch, nor shall he be thrown to the ground after such catch is made unless he has advanced beyond his mark.

SUGGESTION.—This rule does not forbid a player who is on-side from interfering with a fair catch. How often it occurs that such opportunities are missed by players who are on-side; they do not realize that they have just as much right to that ball as the player making the fair catch. When the opponents are attempting a fair catch, after a kick-off, kick-out, punt-out, kick from a fair catch, both sides are on-side and any one may secure the ball or interfere with any one else securing it, since all are on-side.

Putting Ball in Play After Fair Catch.

(*b*) If a side obtains a fair catch, the ball must be put in play by a punt, drop-kick or place-kick, and the opponents cannot come within ten yards of the line on which the fair catch was made; the ball must be kicked from some point directly behind the spot where the catch was made, on a line parallel to the side line.

RULE 8.

REFEREE HAS JURISDICTION.

Goal.

A *Goal* is made by kicking the ball in any way, except by a punt, from the field of play over the cross-bar of the opponents' goal, or as provided in rules for conversion of touchdown. If the ball passes directly over one of the uprights it counts a goal.

NOTE—If the ball, after being kicked, strikes an opponent and then passes over the cross-bar, it still counts a goal.

SUGGESTION.—A ball kicked from the field of play in *any way*, except by a punt over the cross-bar of the opponents' goal, is a goal under the above rule. If the ball was lying free on the ground and any player on-side kicked it and it went across the goal bar it would be a goal.

RULE 9.

UMPIRE HAS JURISDICTION.

Charging.

Charging is rushing forward to seize or block the ball or to tackle a player.

RULE 10.

UMPIRE HAS JURISDICTION OF EACH SECTION.

Off-side.
PENALTY, 5 yards.

(*a*) In a scrimmage no part of any player shall be ahead of the ball when it is put in play. [Exception under Rule 6 (*c*).]

NOTE—Ahead of the ball means between the opponents' goal and a line parallel to the goal line and passing through the point of the ball nearest to the goal line of the side not in possession.

No player shall be out of bounds at the time when the ball is put in play, save as provided for elsewhere in these rules. (See Rule 25, section *c*.)

Player Put Off-side.

(*b*) A player is put off-side if the ball in play has last been touched by one of his own side behind him. No player, when off-side, shall touch the ball except on a fumble or a muff, nor shall he interrupt or obstruct an opponent with his hands or arms until again on-side. [This shall not be so interpreted as to prevent a man who is running down the field under a kick from using his hands or arms to push opponents out of the way in order to get at the ball or the man catching it.] No player can, however, be called off-side behind his own goal line.

Kicked Ball Strikes Player Off-side.

NOTE—If a player is ahead of the ball when it is kicked by another of his side, he is off-side, and he shall not allow the ball to touch him until again on-side. Should he break this rule, the ball goes to opponents on the spot, except as specified in (d) of this rule.

Player Off-side Put On-side.

(c) A player being off-side is put on-side when the ball has touched an opponent, or when one of his own side has run in front of him, either with the ball, or having been the last player to touch it when behind him.

The man who, standing back of his own line of scrimmage receives the ball from one of his own side and then kicks it beyond the line of scrimmage, may not put other men on-side by running ahead of them, nor may he himself get the ball until after it has touched a player of the opposing side.

EXPLANATION—The Rules Committee desires to state that the reason for this prohibition is in order that there may be no excuse whatever for running into the fullback after he has kicked the ball. The above rule renders it impossible for him either to put men on-side or himself get the ball, and this takes away all excuse for roughness of this nature, and the Committee expects officials to severely punish any such unnecessary roughness.

SUGGESTION.—This rule does not prohibit any one from securing a ball after he has kicked it, unless he has received it and made a scrimmage kick. If he returned a punt from an opponent's kick, a kick-off of an opponent, or a place-kick of an opponent, the kicker would be on-side and could go and secure the ball before an opponent touched it, and not violate this rule.

Ball Inside 10-yard Line Touched by a Player Who Is Off-side.

(d) If the ball, when not in possession of either side, is

touched when inside the opponents' 10-yard line by a player who is off-side, it is a foul, and the penalty is that it shall go as a touchback to the defenders of that goal.

RULE 11.

REFEREE HAS JURISDICTION OF EACH SECTION.

Ball Is Dead.

The ball is *Dead:*

(*a*) Whenever the referee blows his whistle or declares a down.

(*b*) Whenever the referee has declared that a down, touch-down, touchback, safety or goal has been made.

(*c*) When a fair catch has been heeled.

(*d*) When it has been downed after going out of bounds.

(*e*) When the ball goes out of bounds after a kick before touching a player who is on-side.

If the umpire signals a foul, the play continues until the ball is dead under some of the above provisions, when the referee must enforce the penalty called for by the umpire's decision. The side offended may, however, refuse to accept the penalty.

NOTE—(a) Should the ball strike an official it is not regarded as dead, but play continues exactly as if the ball had not touched him.

(b) No play can be made when the ball is dead, except to put it in play according to rule.

RULE 12.

REFEREE HAS JURISDICTION OF EACH SECTION.

Length of Game.

(*a*) The length of the game shall be 70 minutes, divided into two halves of 35 minutes each, exclusive of time taken out. There shall be ten minutes intermission between the two halves.

NOTE—The game may be of shorter duration by mutual agreement between the captains of the contesting teams.

Darkness.

Whenever the commencement of a game is so late that, in the opinion of the referee, there is any likelihood of the game being interfered with by darkness, he shall, before play begins, arbitrarily shorten the two halves to such length as shall insure two equal halves being completed, and shall notify both captains of the exact time thus set. Either side refusing to abide by the opinion of the referee on this point shall forfeit the game.

Final Score.

(*b*) The game shall be decided by the final score at the end of the two halves.

Time Called at End of a Half.

(*c*) Time shall not be called for the end of a half until the ball is dead, and in case of a touchdown, the try-at-goal shall be allowed.

Time Taken Out.

(*d*) Time shall be taken out whenever the game is unnecessarily delayed or while the ball is being brought out for a try-at-goal, kick-out, or kick-off, or when play is for any reason suspended by the referee. Time shall be taken out after a fair catch. Time shall begin again when the ball is actually put in play.

NOTE:—Time is not to be taken out when the ball goes out of bounds except in case of unreasonable delay in returning the ball to play.

No Delay Longer Than Two Minutes.

PENALTY, five yards for any unnecessary delay. Refusing to play within two minutes after ordered by referee to do so shall forfeit the game.

(*e*) No delay arising from any cause whatsoever shall continue more than two minutes. Any unreasonable delay shall be penalized under Rule 28 (*A* and *D*), and persistent delay shall be penalized as provided for in Penalties—*D*.

RULE 13.

REFEREE HAS JURISDICTION.

Beginning of Game and of Second Half.

(*a*) The captains of the opposing teams shall toss up a coin before the beginning of a game, and the winner of the toss shall have his choice of goal or kick-off. If the winner of the toss selects the goal, the loser must take the kick-off. The ball shall be kicked off at the beginning of each half, the kick-off at the beginning of the second half being made by the side that did not first kick off at the beginning of the game. The teams shall change goals after every try-at-goal following a touchdown, and after every goal from the field, and the side just scored upon shall have the option of kicking off or of having their opponents kick off. At the beginning of the second half the teams shall take opposite goals from those assumed at the beginning of the first half.

REFEREE HAS JURISDICTION.

Ball Kicked Out of Bounds at Kick-off.

(b) At kick-off, if the ball goes out of bounds before it is touched by an opponent, it shall be brought back and kicked off again. If it is kicked out of bounds a second time it shall go as a kick-off to the opponents. If either side thus forfeits the ball twice, it shall go to the opponents, who shall put it in play by a scrimmage at the center of the field.

REFEREE HAS JURISDICTION.

Ball Kicked Across Goal Line at Kick-off.

(c) At kick-off, or at any other time, if the ball is kicked across the goal line and is there declared dead when in the possession of one of the side defending the goal, it is a touchback. If the ball is not declared dead, the side defending the goal may run with it or kick it exactly as if it had not crossed the goal line. If it is declared dead thus in possession of the attacking side, provided that the man was on-side, it is a touchdown.

UMPIRE HAS JURISDICTION.

Position of Opponents at Kick-out and Kick From Fair Catch.

(d) At kick-off and on a punt or drop-kick from a fair catch, the opposite side must stand at least 10 yards in front of the ball until it is kicked. On a kick-out, the opposite side cannot stand nearer the goal than the 25-yard line, except on a kick-out made after a try at field goal from scrimmage upon a first down inside the 25-yard line, when the 10-yard line is the restraining mark. [See Rule 23, exception.]

RULE 14.

Umpire Has Jurisdiction.

Position on Free-kick.

(*a*) The side which has a free-kick must be behind the ball when it is kicked.

NOTE—Otherwise the kick must be made again under conditions laid down in Penalties—H.

Referee Has Jurisdiction.

Must Kick Ball 10 Yards.

(*b*) In the case of a kick-off, kick-out, kick from a fair catch, the ball must be kicked a distance of at least 10 yards towards the opponents' goal from the line restraining the player making the kick, unless it is stopped by an opponent; otherwise the ball is not in play.

Suggestion.—In case a short kick is made by your side on a kick-off, kick-out or kick from a fair catch, and the ball does not go ten yards, fall on it. Do not let the opponents secure it, as it will be in play if they do, and you will not have an opportunity to kick off again, which you will have if you fall on it before it has gone ten yards.

RULE 15.

Umpire Has Jurisdiction of Each Section.

Lawful Charging.

(*a*) Charging is lawful, in case of a punt-out or kick-off, as soon as the ball is kicked; and the opponents must not charge until the ball is kicked.

Ball Touching the Ground by Accident.

(*b*) In case of any other free-kick, charging is lawful: (1) When the player of the side having the free-kick advances beyond his restraining line or mark with the ball in his possession; (2) If he allows the ball to touch the ground by accident or otherwise.

After Lawful Charging Ball Must Be Kicked.

(*c*) If such lawful charging takes place, and if the side having the free-kick fails to kick the ball, then the opponents may line up 5 yards ahead of the line which restrained them before charging. In that case, the side having the free-kick must kick the ball from some point directly behind its mark, if the free-kick resulted from a fair catch, and in other cases from behind the new restraining line.

EXCEPTION—If, in case of a try-at-goal, after a touchdown, the ball is not kicked, after having been allowed to touch the ground once, no second attempt shall be permitted, and the ball shall be kicked off at the center of the field. (Rule 13.)

RULE 16.

REFEREE HAS JURISDICTION.

No Interference with Snapper-back.

PENALTY, 5 yards.

(*a*) The snapper-back is entitled to full and undisturbed possession of the ball. The opponents must neither interfere with the snapper-back nor touch the ball until it is actually put in play.

UMPIRE HAS JURISDICTION.

Snapper-back Off-side.

(*b*) In snapping the ball back, if the player so doing is off-side, the ball must be snapped again, and if this occurs once more on the same down, the opponents shall receive 5 yards, the number of the down and the point to be gained remaining unchanged. If the player is off-side for the third time on the same scrimmage the ball shall go to the opponents.

UMPIRE HAS JURISDICTION.

(*c*) The man who snaps back and the man opposite him in the scrimmage may not afterward touch the ball until it has touched some player other than these two. If this rule is broken, the side infringing shall be set back 5 yards and the ball put in play again by the same side that had it, the number of the down and the point to be gained remaining the same.

UMPIRE HAS JURISDICTION.

Restrictions When Ball Is Put in Play by Kick Forward.

(*d*) If the man who puts the ball in play in a scrimmage kicks it forward, no player of his side can touch it until it has gone 10 yards into the opponents' territory, unless it be touched by an opponent. If this rule is broken the ball goes to the opponents on the spot of the foul.

REFEREE HAS JURISDICTION.

Advance of Ball by Player First Receiving It From Snapper-back.

PENALTY, 15 yards.

(*c*) The man who first receives the ball when it is snapped back shall not (save as provided in Rule 18, *c*) carry the ball forward beyond the line of scrimmage unless he has regained it after it has been passed to and has touched another player.

RULE 17.

UMPIRE HAS JURISDICTION OF EACH SECTION.

No Interference with Opponents Before Ball Is in Play.

PENALTY, 5 yards.

(*a*) Before the ball is put in play no player shall lay his hands upon, or by the use of his hands or arms, interfere with an opponent in such a way as to delay putting the ball in play. Any such interference shall be regarded as delay of game. (Rule 28, *A*.)

No Use of Hands or Arms by Attacking Side.

PENALTY, 5 yards.

(*b*) After the ball is put in play, the players of the side that has possession of the ball may obstruct the opponents with the body only, except the player running with the ball, who may use his hands and arms.

Defending Side May Use Hands and Arms.

PENALTY, 5 yards.

(*c*) The players of the side not having the ball may use their hands and arms, but only to get their opponents out of the way in order to reach the ball or stop the player carrying it.

Use of hand to ward off tackler.

RULE 18.

UMPIRE HAS JURISDICTION.

Movement Allowed Before Ball Is Put in Play.

PENALTY, 5 yards.

(*a*) Before the ball is put in play in a scrimmage, if any

player of the side which has the ball takes more than one step in any direction, he must come to a full stop before the ball is put in play.

EXCEPTION—One man of the side having the ball may be in motion towards his own goal without coming to a stop before the ball is put in play.

Umpire Has Jurisdiction.

Penalty, 5 yards.

(*b*) At least six men of the side holding the ball must be on the line of scrimmage. If not more than six men are on the line of scrimmage one man of those not on the scrimmage line must be outside the position occupied by the man on the end of the line. The line of scrimmage is an imaginary line parallel to the goal line and passing through the front point of the ball. A player shall be considered to be on the line of scrimmage if he has his head, his foot, or his hand up to or within one foot of this line. He must also, however, be outside the player next and between him and the snapper-back. In this rule "outside" means both feet outside the outside foot of the player next and between him and the snapper-back, as aforesaid.

Referee Has Jurisdiction.

Penalty, 15 yards.

(*c*) The first man receiving the ball from the snapper-back may carry the ball forward, provided he crosses the line of scrimmage at least 5 yards outside of the point where the ball was snapped.

Suggestion.—This rule permits any player to run with a ball on a direct pass from center. So many teams get the idea that only quarter-backs may run on a direct pass.

RULE 19.

Referee Has Jurisdiction.

Throwing, Passing or Batting the Ball.

Penalty, 5 yards.

A player may throw, pass or bat the ball in any direction except toward his opponents' goal.

RULE 20.

Referee Has Jurisdiction.

A Down.

(*a*) If a player having the ball is tackled, and the movement of the ball stopped, or if the player cries "down," the referee shall blow his whistle, and the side holding the ball shall put it down for scrimmage.

Referee Has Jurisdiction.

(*b*) As soon as a runner attempting to go through is tackled and goes down, being held by an opponent, or whenever a runner having the ball in his possession cries "down," or if he goes out of bounds, the referee shall blow his whistle and the ball shall be considered down at that spot.

Umpire Has Jurisdiction.

No Piling Up on Player.

Penalty, 5 yards.

(*c*) There shall be no piling up on the player after the referee has declared the ball dead.

NOTE—In order to prevent the prevalent stealing of the ball, the referee shall blow his whistle immediately when the forward progress of the ball has been stopped.

RULE 21.

Referee Has Jurisdiction of Each Section.

Necessary Gain in Three Downs.

(*a*) If, in three consecutive downs (unless the ball crosses the goal line), a team has not advanced the ball 5 yards, it shall go to the opponents on the spot of the fourth down.

"Consecutive" Downs.

NOTE—"Consecutive" means without going out of possession of the side holding it, except that—(1) having advanced the ball beyond the point necessary for the first down or the ball having actually passed into possession of the other side and then been fumbled and lost by them before having been declared dead by the referee; or, (2) by having kicked the ball they have given their opponents fair and equal chance of gaining possession of it. No kick,

Kicked Ball Must Go Beyond Line of Scrimmage.

however, provided it is not stopped by an opponent, is regarded as giving the opponents fair and equal chance of possession unless the ball goes beyond the line of scrimmage.

(*b*) When a distance penalty is given, the ensuing down shall be counted, as provided for under Penalties—*F*.

RULE 22.

Referee Has Jurisdiction.

Putting Ball in Play From Out of Bounds.

If the ball goes out of bounds, whether it bounds back or not, a player of the side which secures it must bring it to the spot where the line was crossed, and there walk out with it at right angles to the side-line, any distance not less than 5 nor more than 15 yards, and at that point put it down for a scrimmage, first declaring how far he intends walking.

Suggestion.—Time is not out when the ball goes out of bounds, so all the men on the defense, when the ball is being brought in, should watch out for a quick play or a long pass.

RULE 23.

Referee Has Jurisdiction (except as relates to position of players, of which umpire has charge).

Kick-out After Safety or Touchback.

A side which has made a touchback or a safety must kick out. from not more than 25 yards outside the kicker's goal. If the ball goes out of bounds before striking a player, it must be kicked out again, and if this occurs twice in succession, it shall be given to

Positions of Opponents at Kick-out.

the opponents as out of bounds on the 35-yard line on the side where it went out. At kick-out the opponents must be on the 25-yard line or nearer their own goal, and the kicker's side must be behind the ball when it is kicked. Should a second touchback occur before four downs have been played, the side defending the goal may have the choice of a down at the 25-yard line, or a kick-out.

If Second Touchback Before Four Downs.

In case of a second failure to kick within bounds the ball shall go to the opponents on the 25-yard line.

After Drop-kick at Goal on First Down Inside 25 Yards, Kick-off From 10-yard Line.

EXCEPTION—Whenever a side has tried a drop-kick or a place-kick from scrimmage at the goal upon a first down inside the 25-yard line and the result has been a touchback, the 10-yard, instead of the 25-yard line, shall determine the position of the opponents, and the kicker's side must be behind the ball when it is kicked.

RULE 24.

REFEREE HAS JURISDICTION OF EACH SECTION.

Try-at-goal After Touchdown.

(a) A side which has made a touchdown must try at goal by a place-kick direct, or by a place-kick preceded by a punt-out if they so desire.

After Touchdown, Defenders Kick Off.

(b) After the try-at-goal, whether the goal be made or missed, the ball shall be kicked off at the center of the field, as provided in Rule 13.

RULE 25.

REFEREE HAS JURISDICTION OF EACH SECTION (except as relates to positions of players and interference).

Try-at-goal by Place-kick.

(a) If the try be a place-kick, a player on the side which has made the touchdown shall hold the ball for another of his side to kick at some point outside the goal on a line parallel to the side line passing through the point where the touchdown was declared. The opponents must remain behind their goal line until the ball has been placed upon the ground. The referee shall signal with his hand when the ball is placed on the ground.

Punt-out Preceding Try-at-goal.

(*b*) If the try-at-goal is to be preceded by a punt-out, the punter shall kick the ball from the point at which the line parallel to the side-line, and passing through the spot of the touchdown, intersects the goal line. The players of his side must stand in the field of play not less than 5 yards from the goal line.

Positions of Players at Punt-out.

The opponents may line up anywhere on the goal line except within the space of 15 feet on each side of the punter's mark, but they shall not interfere with the punter. If a fair catch is made from a punt-out, the mark shall serve to determine the positions as the mark of any fair catch, and the try-at-goal shall then be made by a place-kick from this spot, or any point directly behind it. If a fair catch is not made on the first attempt the ball shall go as a kick-off at the center of the field to the defenders of the goal.

Defending Side May Charge.

NOTE—Since the defending team is on-side, they may, of course, charge as soon as the ball is kicked and try to get the ball or interfere with the catch.

Holder of Ball May Be Off-side.

(*c*) The holder of the ball and no other player in a place-kick from a fair catch or touchdown may be off-side or out of bounds without vitiating the kick.

RULE 26.

REFEREE HAS JURISDICTION.

Scoring.

The following shall be the values of plays in scoring: Goal

obtained by touchdown, 6 points; goal from field-kick, either a drop-kick or place-kick, 4 points; touchdown failing goal, 5 points; safety by opponents, 2 points.

NOTE—The 6 points is inclusive of the 5 points for touchdown; that is, kicking the goal adds but 1 point.

RULE 27.

UMPIRE HAS JURISDICTION.

No Metallic Substances May Be Worn.

PENALTY, disqualification, unless fault corrected within two minutes.

(*a*) No one having projecting nails or iron plates on his shoes or any projecting metallic or hard substance on his person shall be allowed to play in a match. If head protectors are worn, no sole leather, papier mache, or other hard or unyielding material shall be used in their construction, and all other devices for protectors must be so arranged and padded as, in the judgment of the umpire, to be without danger to other players. Leather cleats upon the shoes shall be allowed as heretofore.

UMPIRE HAS JURISDICTION.

Substitutes.

(*b*) A player may be substituted for another at any time at the discretion of the captain of his team.

NOTE—When a substitute is sent in he must go directly to the referee and report himself before taking his place.

UMPIRE HAS JURISDICTION.

No Striking or Unnecessary Roughness.

PENALTY, disqualification.

REFEREE SHALL VOLUNTEER TESTIMONY, ALSO LINESMAN.

(*c*) There shall be no unnecessary roughness, throttling, hacking or striking with the closed fist.

Umpire Has Jurisdiction.

(*d*) A player who has been replaced by a substitute cannot return to further participation in the game.

Referee Has Jurisdiction.

No Unnecessary Delay.

(*e*) There shall be no unnecessary delay of the game by either team.

Umpire Has Jurisdiction.

No Coaching.

Referee Shall Volunteer Testimony, Also Linesman.

(*f*) There shall be no coaching, either by substitutes or by any other persons not participating in the game. In case of accident to a player one representative of the player's team may, if he first obtained the consent of the umpire, come upon the field of play to attend to the injured player. This representative need not always be the same person. No person other than the players, the officials, the representatives above mentioned or an incoming substitute shall at any time come upon the field of play. Only five men shall be allowed to walk up and down on each side of the field. The rest, including substitutes, water carriers, and all who are admitted within the enclosure, must be seated throughout the game. Breach of any part of this rule shall constitute a foul, and be punished by a loss of 10 yards to the side whose man infringes, the number of the down and the distance to be gained for first down remaining unchanged. See, however, Rule 28 *J*.

NOTE:—The Rules Committee especially requests the captains and coaches to use every means to discourage and prevent sideline coaching.

Umpire Has Jurisdiction.

No Tripping.

Penalty, 15 yards.

(*g*) There shall be no tripping.

RULE 28.

PENALTIES.

A Foul is any violation of a rule. The penalties for fouls shall be as follows:

A. Loss of 5 Yards.

1. Coaching or infringement of any part of Rule 27, *f*.
2. Delay of game (Rule 12, *e*; Rule 17, *a*).
3. Interference with putting ball in play (Rule 16, *a*).
4. Off-side in scrimmage (Rule 10, *a*).
5. Starting before ball (Rule 18).
6. Scrimmage rule violated (Rule 18).
7. Snapper-back off-side second time in same down. (For third offense on same down the ball goes to opponents.) (Rule 16, *b*.)
8. Passing or batting ball forward (Rule 19).
9. Unsportsmanlike conduct (see provision "L," Rule 28).
10. Holding by defensive side of player not carrying the ball (Rule 17, *c*).
11. Snapper-back or man opposite touching ball before it has touched third man (Rule 16, *c*).
12. Piling up after the ball has been declared dead (Rule 20, *c*).

B. Loss of 15 Yards.

1. Tripping (Rule 27, *g*).
2. Holding or illegal use of hands or arms by team in possession of ball (Rule 17, *b*).
3. Illegal running by man receiving ball directly from snapper-back (Rules 16, *e;* 18).
4. Interference with fair catch (see provision "G," Rule 28).

C. Disqualification.

1. Unnecessary roughness, throttling, hacking or striking with closed fist (Rule 27, *c*).
2. Violation of Rule 27, *a*, unless the fault is corrected within two minutes.

D. Forfeiture of Game.

1. Refusing to play within two minutes after having been ordered by the referee to do so. (Rule 12, *e*.)
2. Defensive team committing fouls so near their goal line that these fouls are punishable only by halving the distance to the

goal line in order. in the opinion of the referee, to delay the game. (The referee shall warn offending side once before declaring game forfeited.) (See Rule 28—*K.*)

RULINGS IN CONNECTION WITH PENALTIES

E. When a foul has been committed and a signal to that effect has been given by the umpire or linesman, each acting within the limit of his authority as given under Duties of Officials, the referee shall call the ball back to the spot where the foul was committed and from that point exact the penalty as prescribed above.

When a foul has been declared the ball may not be again put in play until the penalty has been exacted or declined. (See next provision.)

The offended side may decline to accept the penalty, in which case play is resumed exactly as if no foul occurred.

SUGGESTION.—The last paragraph makes it possible for the offended side to refuse any penalty. If they do, they can have the advantage of anything that resulted from the play on which the penalty was given.

F. Whenever a distance penalty has been given the ball shall be put in play by a scrimmage unless otherwise specifically provided for by the rules. This scrimmage shall be counted as first down if the offense was committed by the side not in possession of the ball. In case the side in possession of the ball was the offender the down and point to be gained for first down shall remain the same as they were at the beginning of the scrimmage during which the foul occurred.

EXCEPTION—If the foul was committed after a gain of such length that after the exaction of the distance penalty the ball is still in advance of the point necessary for first down when he ball was last put in play, the ensuing down shall be counted the first down, with five yards to gain for the next first down.

In case neither side was in possession of the ball when the foul was committed—for example, if the ball was in the air or free upon the ground after a kick, fumble or poor pass—it shall go to the offended side as first down at the spot where the foul occurred.

Under this head would come the following:

1. In case of scrimmage kick on third down, the kicking side touching the ball after the kick before it passed the line of scrimmage (Rule 21).

2. Touching ball after a kick when player is off-side. (Ex-

cept inside opponents' 10-yard line, when a touchback shall be declared.) (Rule 10, *b* and *d*.)

3. If ball not in possession is batted forward (Rule 19).

4. In case of tripping, the distance penalty shall be given in addition.

G. If a player who has an opportunity of making a fair catch (Rule 7) is unlawfully obstructed by an opponent who is off-side and thus prevented from catching the ball, or if a player who has heeled a fair catch is thrown to the ground (unless he has advanced beyond his mark) his side shall have the choice of two penalties, viz. :—

1. They may receive 15 yards, in which case they must put the ball in play by a scrimmage; or,

2. They may receive 5 yards, in which case they must put the ball in play by a punt, drop-kick or place-kick.

H. In any case of free-kick (Rule 2, *f*, and 15, *b*) if the kicker advances beyond his mark before kicking the ball, no matter whether he then kicks it or not, the opponents shall be allowed to line up 5 yards nearer the kicker's mark, and the kick shall then be made from some point back of the first mark and at the same distance from the side line.

This shall also apply when the side having a free-kick allows the ball to touch the ground (Rule 15, *b;* Rule 25, *b*) and then fails to kick it (kick-off and try-at-goal after touchdown excepted). The same ruling shall be given in case any player of the side making a free-kick is ahead of the ball when it is kicked (Rule 14, *a*).

I. In the case of a free-kick, if the opponents charge before the ball is put in play (Rule 13, *d*) they shall be put back 5 yards for every such offense and the ball shall be put in play again by a kick from a point which may be 5 yards nearer the opponents' goal if the kicking side so desire.

NOTE—In case a team is penalized under this rule at or near their goal line, e. g., in case of illegal charging during a try-for-goal after touchdown or throwing the catcher of a punt-out, the regular penalty shall be exacted even though it results in placing them behind their own goal line. A second offense here shall be penalized exactly as if it had occurred outside the goal line.

J. Whenever the rules provide for a distance penalty, if the distance prescribed would carry the ball nearer to the goal line than the 5-yard line, the ball shall be down on the 5-yard line. If, however, the foul was committed inside the 10-yard line, half the distance to the goal line shall be given.

K. If a team on the defense commits fouls so near their own goal that these fouls are punishable only by halving of the distance to the line, the object being, in the opinion of the referee, to delay the game, the offending side shall be regarded as refusing to allow the game to proceed. The referee shall in such cases warn the offending side once and if the offense is repeated, he shall declare the game forfeited to the opponents.

L. In case the game is interfered with by some act palpably unsportsmanlike and not elsewhere provided for in these rules, the umpire shall have the power to award 5 yards to the offended side, the number of the down and the point to be gained for first down being determined as provided for in "F."

Pulling the runner along for extra yards.

Also from Benediction Books ...

Wandering Between Two Worlds: Essays on Faith and Art
Anita Mathias
Benediction Books, 2007
152 pages
ISBN: 0955373700

Available from www.amazon.com, www.amazon.co.uk
www.wanderingbetweentwoworlds.com

In these wide-ranging lyrical essays, Anita Mathias writes, in lush, lovely prose, of her naughty Catholic childhood in Jamshedpur, India; her large, eccentric family in Mangalore, a sea-coast town converted by the Portuguese in the sixteenth century; her rebellion and atheism as a teenager in her Himalayan boarding school, run by German missionary nuns, St. Mary's Convent, Nainital; and her abrupt religious conversion after which she entered Mother Teresa's convent in Calcutta as a novice. Later rich, elegant essays explore the dualities of her life as a writer, mother, and Christian in the United States-- Domesticity and Art, Writing and Prayer, and the experience of being "an alien and stranger" as an immigrant in America, sensing the need for roots.

About the Author

Anita Mathias was born in India, has a B.A. and M.A. in English from Somerville College, Oxford University and an M.A. in Creative Writing from the Ohio State University. Her essays have been published in The Washington Post, The London Magazine, The Virginia Quarterly Review, Commonweal, Notre Dame Magazine, America, The Christian Century, Religion Online, The Southwest Review, Contemporary Literary Criticism, New Letters, The Journal, and two of HarperSanFrancisco's The Best Spiritual Writing anthologies. Her non-fiction has won fellowships from The National Endowment for the Arts; The Minnesota State Arts Board; The Jerome Foundation, The Vermont Studio Center; The Virginia Centre for the Creative Arts, and the First Prize for the Best General Interest Article from the Catholic Press Association of the United States and Canada. Anita has taught Creative Writing at the College of William and Mary, and now lives and writes in Oxford, England.

www.ingramcontent.com/pod-product-compliance
Lightning Source LLC
Chambersburg PA
CBHW030638150426
42813CB00050B/117